WINCHESTER SCHOOL OF MISSION

08303

The Way of a Pilgrim

D1340629

The Way of a Pilgrim

Annotated & Explained

Translation & annotation
by Gleb Pokrovsky

DARTON·LONGMAN + TODD

First published in Great Britain in 2003 by
Darton, Longman and Todd Ltd
1 Spencer Court
140–142 Wandsworth High Street
London SW18 4JJ

First published in the USA in 2001 by
SkyLight Paths Publishing
a division of LongHill Partners, Inc.
Sunset Farm Offices, Route 4, P.O. Box 237
Woodstock, VT 05091

© 2001 SkyLight Paths Publishing

Material on pages 42 and 52 from *The Philokalia: The Complete Text*, vol. 1, translated by G.E.H. Palmer, Philip Sherrard, and Kallistos Ware, translation © 1979 by the Eling Trust, is used by permission of Faber & Faber Ltd and of Faber and Faber, Inc., an affiliate of Farrar, Straus and Giroux, LLC.

The right of Gleb Pokrovsky to be identified as the translator and annotator of this work has been asserted in accordance with the Copyright, Designs and Patents Act 1988.

ISBN 0–232–52475–0

A catalogue record for this book is available from the British Library.

Text design by Chelsea Cloeter

Printed and bound in Great Britain by
Page Bros, Norwich, Norfolk

Contents ◻

Foreword ▢

Andrew Harvey

Some books come to mean so much to you that you never forget the first time you read them. The first time I read *The Way of a Pilgrim* was over twenty years ago. I was then an academic, a fellow of an Oxford college; I had just returned to England after a life-changing year-long stay in India where, for the first time, I had become aware of mystical reality through a series of experiences I could neither explain nor deny. I came back to Oxford convinced that spiritual truth could only be found in India and the Eastern spiritual traditions, and that Christianity was "finished" and "burned out."

The first person I imposed my new vision on was my best friend, Anne Pennington, a professor of Slavonic studies and a devout Russian Orthodox Christian. Anne listened patiently to my Indian raptures but cut me short when I started to dismiss the whole of Western religious experience. "How can you judge the Christian mystical tradition by what you see in the contemporary church?" she said. "That would be like judging the entire tradition of classical music by the dissonant ravings of the latest so-called 'composer.' When you're settled in and less stubborn, I'm going to send you a book that will change your mind. And perhaps not only your mind. . . ."

The book she sent me was her own worn and annotated copy of *The Way of a Pilgrim* along with photocopies of her favorite quotes on the prayer of the heart from the *Philokalia*, the famous anthology of Eastern Orthodox texts on the spiritual life. It was a glowing, golden September,

I remember: I took the book and the quotes out into a garden by the river and devoured them there in one sitting, transfixed and humbled by what I found. In India I had encountered for the first time the practice of *japa*—of repeating the name of God in the heart—and now I realized that in the Jesus prayer, "Lord Jesus Christ, have mercy on me," the Eastern Orthodox tradition had made the same simple, all-transforming discovery of the power of the divine name. The ecstasies and revelations of the anonymous narrator of *The Way of a Pilgrim* were no less profound and poignant than those that had so shaken me in Mirabai, Kabir, and Toukaram, the great Hindu and Sufi mystics the discovery of whom had changed my life. And in the string of quotes from the *Philokalia*—from figures such as Symeon the New Theologian, Isaac the Syrian, and Gregory Palamas—then totally unknown to me—I recognized the pure sober note of mystical certainty and rigor that had thrilled me in the *Bhagavad Gita* and the Upanishads. A week later at dinner Anne and I discussed the practice of the Jesus prayer. I asked Anne what it meant to her. She paused a long time and then answered softly, "Everything." Two years later when she was dying of cancer, still only in her forties, I asked her what was sustaining her faith and courage. "The Jesus prayer," she replied. "It gives me everything I need." After her death, I had a dream of her standing, flooded by divine light, by a statue of the resurrected Christ. She was gazing at me with immense tenderness and some amusement as if to say, "And now do you at last understand how powerful prayer of the heart can be?" In her right hand, she was holding the copy of *The Way of a Pilgrim* she had lent me.

Although it would be ten more years before I set about practicing the Jesus prayer seriously, I can now say with wonder and gratitude that I am beginning to know what Anne was so anxious to show me. There are many ways you can read this profound and glorious book that is one of the world's religious masterpieces. Whatever path you find yourself on, you can revel in it as a spiritual adventure story, the account of a man who searches for the meaning of prayer and mystical truth and finds them on a journey peppered with colorful encounters, visions, and those reveal-ing twists of fate of which any sincere seeker's life is full. If you are a practicing mystic, you can read *The Way of a Pilgrim* as a skillful and wise presentation of the theory and practice of the Jesus prayer, taking to heart its instructions and precise advice, delighting in the many subtle ways it opens up to you the treasures of the Eastern Orthodox tradition. I have known Hindus who have been inspired to return to their own prac-tice by it and Buddhists who have found in its pages deep confirmation of their own experience of meditation. If you are not religious at all, you can enjoy *The Way of a Pilgrim* as a brilliantly sensuous and pungent evo-cation of mid–nineteenth-century Russia, with its villages and mud roads, snowy wastes and vast virgin forests, and that all-rewarding atmosphere of religious passion that permeates Russian literature from its origins through the novels of Tolstoy and Dostoyevsky, right up to the modern works of Pasternak and Solzhenitsyn. One incorrigibly secular friend of mine, a Russian-born philosopher, once surprised me by saying, "The three greatest books in Russian are *War and Peace, The Idiot,* and *The Way of a Pilgrim.*" When I asked him why he had included the latter, he replied, "Because it breathes the rich leather-and-incense perfume of old Russia with unique force." For myself, now, I find that the deeper and most satisfying way of reading *The Way of a Pilgrim* is as the unfolding of a profound mystical initiation into the ecstasy and truth of what Jesus called "the Kingdom," that state of divine knowledge and love that reveals the world as sacred and all beings as inherently divine that is the true goal of the Christian life.

Many readers who come to *The Way of a Pilgrim* for the first time will find as I did, that it has a mysteriously initiatory power. The clue to this power, I believe, is that the work itself unfolds in the rhythms of sacred time and providence, with something of the same unpredictable and para-doxical simplicity of the Divine itself. This initiatory intent is stated early on: When the pilgrim meets the man who will become his *starets,* the old priest explains to him why his attempts up to now to discover the

meaning of "unceasing prayer" have been unsuccessful: "Until now you
have been tested in the cooperation of your will with God's calling and
have been granted to understand that neither the wisdom of this world
nor mere superficial curiosity can attain to the divine illumination of
unceasing interior prayer." And the starets adds, making his meaning even
more clear, "On the contrary, it is the humble simple heart that attains to
such prayer, through poverty of the spirit and a living experience of it."
The entire remainder of the book unveils the radical deepening of the pilgrim's knowledge of poverty of spirit and of the living experience of divine
presence that interior prayer opens him to. From the pivotal meeting with
the starets onward, everything that occurs to the pilgrim occurs in the
rhythms of a secret providence that guides him through both exterior
events and graded stages of inner self-revelation to an ever-more radiant
awareness of the Christ-fire burning within him and in the creation, in all its
tender glory. It is part of the work's enduring magic that so profound a
process should be unfolded in the simplest imaginable prose, with a directness of approach that mirrors the directness of Truth itself. It is this dia-
mantine, Gospel-like simplicity that draws the reader into believing that
what is revealed to and in the pilgrim could be revealed to and in herself.

Central to the mystery of intimacy that *The Way of a Pilgrim* creates
is the naked heartfelt intensity of the pilgrim's voice. From his first words
we realize that we are in the presence of someone whom life and suffering have stripped to his essential core and seared clean of any desire to
impress or convert, someone whose witness, then, to the deepening and
miraculous effects of mystical prayer we can wholly believe. As he tells us,
quite early on, of his experience of the power of the prayer; "There were
days when I covered forty-seven miles or more and I didn't feel the effort
of walking; the prayer alone filled my consciousness. When it was bitterly cold, I would pray more fervently and soon I'd feel warm all over. If
hunger threatened to overcome me, I would call upon the name of Jesus
Christ with renewed vigor and hunger was forgotten." It is the earthy
no-nonsense precision of this testimony that reassures and convinces us,

and helps us identify with the pilgrim with real trust. He speaks to us as a humble brother-in-Christ with such naturalness that the amazing truths he comes to share seem to us, in the end, wholly natural, and something an expanded vision of our own nature, and of the true nature of God and life, could open us to also. It is this naturalness (and the humility that irradiates it) that enables the pilgrim not only to convey to us the depths of his inner experience but also to teach us by example—without in any way imposing this teaching on us—how to work with divine grace. In his ardor, constant receptivity, and exuberant compassion toward all the beings he meets and learns from, the pilgrim becomes a mirror for the best in us, becomes, in a sense, the pilgrim within all of us who longs to find truth and to live a guilelessly divine human life. As *The Way of a Pilgrim* unfolds we see the narrator being fashioned by changing events, the hand of grace, and his own rigorous cooperation with providence, into a true teacher, one whom the Christ has brought into his presence and given the radiant authority of his own direct truth. All the different visions and mystical insights of the pilgrim's journey culminate toward the end of the book in his wonderful experience at Tobolsk:

> The prayer of the heart delighted me so much that I thought there could be no one happier than me in the whole world and I could not imagine how there would be any great or deeper contentment even in the Kingdom of Heaven. Not only did I experience all this within myself, but outwardly as well— everything around me appeared wondrous to me and inspired me with love for and gratitude to God. People, trees, plants and animals—I felt a kinship with them all and discovered how each bore the seal of the Name of Jesus Christ. At times I felt so light it was as if I had no body and were not walking but rather joyously floating through the air. At other times I entered so fully into myself that I saw clearly all my inner organs, and this caused me to marvel at the wisdom that went into creating the human body. Sometimes I knew such joy that

I felt like a king. At such consoling moments I wished that God would grant me to die soon, so that I could pour myself out in gratitude at His feet in heaven.

We believe in the pilgrim's awe-inspiring vision not only because of the dazzled and humble way in which he transmits it to us but also because, immediately afterwards, he confesses, "It became apparent to me that my enjoyment of these experiences was tempered or had been regulated by God's will," and goes on to tell us of a period of anxiety and fear which humbles him and deepens his awareness of what a true teacher has to accept and understand:

> Clouds of thoughts descended upon my mind and I remem-
> bered the words of the blessed John of Kapathos who said that
> often the teacher submits to humiliation and suffers misfor-
> tune and temptations for those who will benefit from him spir-
> itually. After struggling for a while with such thoughts, I began
> to pray earnestly, and the thoughts were banished entirely. I
> was encouraged by this and said to myself, "God's will be
> done! Anything that Jesus Christ may send my way I am ready
> to endure for my wretchedness and arrogance—for even those
> to whom I had recently disclosed the secret of entering the
> heart and of interior prayer had been prepared directly by
> God's hidden guidance, before I met them."

By implication, we, the readers who have followed the pilgrim so far into mystery and revelation have also been prepared not by him for the truths he is sharing with us, but by God. At the very moment the narrator could have put us in awe of him and of his search, his wisdom enables him to free himself, and us, from anything but wonder at divine wisdom and mercy. With astounding subtlety, then, the pilgrim shows us how he has been guided—and has guided us—by divine grace from mystical ecstasy into holy sobriety and the all-healing recognition of his (and our) own utter dependence of the Divine. In so doing, the pilgrim reminds us that the Divine will only go on revealing itself to one who remains in awe and adoration and ever-deepening surrender to Its truth.

It is this awe, adoration, and surrender that the last, wild story the pilgrim tells us shows that he has truly begun to live and know. In it he tells us of how he was staying overnight in the hut of a drunken postmaster, whose cook prepares him a bed. The pilgrim is pretending to sleep when suddenly the entire hut is shaken and the window "in the front corner of the house—the frame, the glass, and all—came showering down with a terrible crash;" a carriage has by mistake crashed into the house. At this the peasant cook "sprang back in terror and jumped into the middle of the room, where she went crashing down on the floor." At first the reader has no idea why he is being told such a bizarre story seemingly unconnected to anything that has gone before. A page later we are given the reason: he tells us that six years later he was passing a women's monastery where he was entertained by the abbess and was moved by the humility of the nun pouring him tea—only to discover that this was the same woman he had encountered in the postmaster's hut—the violent experience several years previously having transformed her into a humble God-seeker. The revelation of the wisdom and mercy of divine providence that this story gives him completes and seals the pilgrim's long initiation and he tells us simply: "Upon this my soul rejoiced and glorified God, who so wisely orders all things for the good." His long journey has brought the pilgrim (and us with him) to the point when at last he is humble (and humbled) enough to see the hand of grace in all the tragedies and disasters of the world, and to surrender completely to a mystery he knows he will and can never understand, but he now knows enough to understand it to be a Mystery of Love.

The Way of a Pilgrim ends with the narrator on the threshold of a journey to Jerusalem. In a sense the book ends where language itself ends, on the threshold of the mystery of divine consciousness that the Rhineland mystic John Ruysbroeck called the "holy unknowing of the Dark in which true lovers lose themselves," and that characterizes the beginnings of

Christ-consciousness. We will never know whether or not the pilgrim reached Jerusalem, and in the deepest sense, it does not matter, because we know that he has found the Holy City and the Kingdom within and outside himself, and has helped us to begin to imagine how we also might be led by grace to make the same discovery for ourselves. The silence at the end of *The Way of a Pilgrim* is like the tremendous silences that surround and elevate us at the end of Beethoven's Ninth Symphony or the Bach B Minor Mass. It is a silence that not only rings with the various kinds of music that are consummated in it but seems, momentarily, to call down, to embody and enshrine the Divine presence itself. Only the highest art informed by the deepest spiritual intelligence and love could lead us to a place where all expression and feeling dissolve in wonder.

I dedicate this foreword to my friend Henry Luce III,
in gratitude and love.

Introduction

The book known in English as *The Way of a Pilgrim* was first published in Russia in 1881 under the title *Otkrivenniye rasskazi strannika svoemu dukhovnomu otsu*—a phrase that can be translated as "Intimate Conversations of a Pilgrim with His Spiritual Father." It was very popular spiritual reading in Russia right up until the time of the revolution. It is the first-person account of a *strannik*—one of the wandering pilgrims who were a regular sight in the Russian countryside from medieval times until the Russian Revolution. Its author and the exact place it originated are unknown, and there is even speculation that it may in fact be a work of fiction.* But regardless of its origin, it has come down to us as the most accessible and inspiring presentation of the practice known as *hesychasm*, or "quietness," the way of prayer that has characterized the spirituality of the Eastern Orthodox Church for many centuries.

The Way of a Pilgrim was first published in English in the 1930s, in a translation by R. M. French, under the title by which it has been known ever since. It remained in print throughout the rest of the twentieth century, but the biggest surge in its popularity came with the publication of J. D. Salinger's best-selling novel *Franny and Zooey* in 1961. (One of the novel's principal characters, Franny Glass, is obsessed with *The Way of a Pilgrim* and with the practice of the Jesus prayer.) Since the 1960s four different English translations have appeared, and it has become the best-known and most widely read of any book on Russian spirituality.

---

* For an interesting discussion of the history of the text, see Aleksei Pentkovsky's introduction to the T. Allan Smith translation in the Classics of Western Spirituality series (publication information on page 138).

This edition provides an abridged version of the text of *The Way of a Pilgrim* with facing-page commentary to explain the names, references, and other details found in the text. Reading it will enhance your understanding of the text and will enable you to proceed to the companion volume, *The Pilgrim Continues His Way*, with greater understanding, as well to other works on Eastern Orthodox spirituality.

First
Narrative

1 Twenty-fourth Sunday after Pentecost: This would be sometime in the winter, in either January or February. When the pilgrim speaks of the Liturgy, he means the Divine Liturgy of St. John Chrystostom, the chanted Sunday service combining readings from the Gospel and Epistles, with celebration of the Eucharist—the Eastern Orthodox equivalent of the Roman Catholic Mass.

2 The text comes from St. Paul's closing exhortations in 1 Thessalonians in verses 11 through 22: "Therefore, encourage one another and build one another up, just as you are doing. But we beseech you, brethren, to respect those who labor among you and are over you in the Lord and admonish you, and esteem them very highly in love because of their work. Be at peace among yourselves. And we exhort you brethren, admonish the idle, encourage the faint-hearted, help the weak, be patient with them all. See that none of you repays evil for evil, but always seek to do good to one another and to all. Rejoice always, pray constantly, give thanks in all circumstances; for this is the will of God in Christ Jesus for you. Do not quench the spirit, do not despise prophesying, but test everything; hold fast to what is good, abstain from every form of evil" (Revised Standard Version).

3 Ephesians 6:18.

4 1 Timothy 2:8.

By the grace of God I am a Christian, by my actions a great sinner, and by calling a homeless wanderer of the simplest origins, traveling from place to place. My worldly belongings are a knapsack that contains some bread, and a Bible in my breast pocket. That is all.

On the twenty-fourth Sunday after Pentecost[1] I went to church to pray at the Liturgy. During the reading of the Epistle of St. Paul to the Thessalonians, I heard the following words: "Pray without ceasing."[2] The words made an indelible impression on me, and I began to wonder how it was possible to pray unceasingly, since everyone must occupy themselves with other matters as well, in order to make a living and so forth. I looked in the Bible and read for myself what I had heard: that one should "pray without ceasing," "pray at all times in the Spirit,"[3] and "in all places pray with uplifted hands."[4] I thought about this for quite a while but was unable to understand it.

"What should I do?" I thought. "Where will I find someone who can explain this to me? I will visit some of the churches that are renowned for their excellent preachers, and perhaps there it can be explained to me." So I went and I heard many good sermons on prayer. But they all dealt with prayer in general: what it is, why it is needed, and what its fruits are. Yet, nothing was said about how to succeed in prayer. There was a sermon on praying in the Spirit and on unceasing prayer, but no mention was made in it about how to attain to such prayer.

Having heard plenty, without acquiring any understanding of how to pray unceasingly, I gave up on such sermons geared to the ordinary

◆ The nineteenth century was the age of the great Russian literary figures Pushkin, Dostoevsky, and Tolstoy. It was a period of spiritual revival in the Russian Orthodox Church. And its second half was a period of radical social reforms. Before 1860, 45 percent of Russia's people lived in serfdom, a form of slavery, bound to inhabit and work the land on which they were born and bought and sold right along with it. The events portrayed in *The Way of a Pilgrim* are thought to have taken place during the reign of Tsar Alexander II (1855–1881), who, in 1860, liberated the serfs. There is no evidence of the great social upheaval this great change brought about in the pilgrim's narrative, which indicates the events were not likely to have happened much after 1860.

parishoner and resolved, with God's help, to seek an experienced and wise guide who would explain unceasing prayer to me, for I now found myself so irresistibly drawn to learning about it.

I set out and wandered for a long time through different places, all the while continuing to read my Bible faithfully. Everywhere I went, I looked into the whereabouts of a local spiritual director. Eventually I was told that in a certain village there was a landowner who had lived there for a long time and who spent all his time working out his salvation. He had a chapel in his house, and he never went out, but did nothing but pray continually and read spiritual literature. When I heard this, I gave up walking and began running in order to get to this village. When I arrived there, I found the man in question. "What is it that you require of me?" he asked.

"I have heard that you are a man of prayer and wisdom. In the name of God, would you please explain to me the meaning of the Apostle's words 'Pray without ceasing' and how one can achieve this? I want to know this, but I have been utterly unable to understand it!"

He was silent for some moments. Then he looked closely at me and said, "Unceasing interior prayer is the constant striving of the spirit toward God. To succeed in this delightful practice, you must beg the Lord more frequently that He teach you how to pray unceasingly. Pray more and ever more earnestly, and the prayer itself will reveal to you how it can become unceasing. This effort will bear fruit in its own time."

Having said this, he offered me refreshment, gave me money for my journey, and sent me on my way. He did not provide me with an explanation after all.

So I set off again, continuing to think and read and wonder about what the man had told me, and still I could not understand it. Yet, my longing for comprehension was so intense that it kept me awake at night.

5 The pilgrim might have expected to see a monastery in any provincial capital, as well as in any town of size, since many Russian towns and cities actually began their existences as monasteries, the process occurring thus: hermits moved as far as possible away from civilization; communities of monks grew up around the hermits; these communities grew into monasteries. For spiritual and economic reasons, laypeople attached themselves to the monasteries, and towns arose. This model was very prevalent in the settlement of the Russian wilderness.

6 St. Dimitri: Dimitri of Rostov (1651–1709); Russian bishop and prolific spiritual writer. Author of a renowned collection of the lives of the saints.

When I had covered about twelve miles, I came to a large provincial capital, where I saw a monastery.[5] I stopped at the inn and happened to hear that in this monastery there was an exceptionally kind abbot, a prayerful and most hospitable man. I went to see him, and he welcomed me joyfully, sat me down, and offered me refreshment.

"Holy Father," I said, "I do not need food, but I seek your spiritual guidance on what I must do to save myself."

"Well now, what must you do to save yourself? Live according to the commandments, pray to God, and you will be saved!"

"I have heard that one should pray unceasingly," I said, "but I do not know how to do this. I do not even understand what unceasing prayer is. Please explain this to me, Father."

"I don't know, dear brother, how else to advise you. Hmmm, but wait just a moment! I do have a little book that will explain it." He brought me *The Spiritual Education of the Interior Man*, by St. Dimitri.[6] "Here you are," he said. "Read this page."

I began to read the following: "Those words of the Apostle 'pray without ceasing' should be understood in reference to the prayer of the mind, for the mind can always aspire to God and pray to Him without ceasing."

"Would you explain to me the means by which the mind can always aspire to God and pray unceasingly, without being distracted?"

"That requires a great deal of wisdom, except for the one to whom God Himself has granted such a gift," said the abbot. He offered no further explanation.

I spent the night in the monastery. The next morning I thanked the abbot for his kind hospitality and continued on my journey, without really knowing where I was headed. I grieved over my lack of understanding and comforted myself by reading my Bible. In this way I traveled for five days, keeping to the main roads. Finally, on the evening of

7 Schema monk: A monk who has taken solemn or final vows, corresponding roughly to "fully professed" in Western monastic systems. In the Russian system, a monk was first a novice, then a *ryassaphor*—one who wears the cassock-like monastic robe called a *ryassa*; then a schema monk—one who wears yet another outer garment called the *schema*, a kind of cape or cloak. Some monks, usually in old age, took another level of particularly solemn vows involving increased fasting and ascetical practices. These monks were said to be tonsured to the "great schema"—by contrast to which ordinary schema monks were identified as "small schema" monks. The system was somewhat different among Greek monastics.

8 The general rule for guests was that they were welcome to enjoy monastic hospitality for three days. Those who stayed on for a fourth day would be expected to join in the monastery's work, or possibly to join the community as a novice monk.

9 Startsi: Plural of *starets*, Russian translation of the Greek term *geron*, "old man." A senior monk, not necessarily a priest, to whom other monks and laypeople turned for spiritual guidance. This ancient tradition of spiritual eldership had undergone a huge revival by the pilgrim's time. In the nineteenth century and up until the Russian revolution, charismatic and influential startsi were a feature of Russian life, and their influence was often felt far beyond monastery walls.

10 The Fathers: "Fathers of the Church": Christian writers characterized by their antiquity, purity of doctrine, or holiness of life, whose words are especially revered by the Orthodox, as well as by some other Christians. There are no official criteria by which a person is judged worthy of the title "Father," but the term would certainly apply to all the writers anthologized in the *Philokalia* and cited in *The Way of a Pilgrim*.

11 The Liturgy: The Divine Liturgy of St. John Chrysostom. The principal service of the Orthodox Church, celebrated on Sundays as well as on feast days. It consists of hymns, readings from the Gospels and Epistles

the fifth day, an old man who appeared to be some kind of clergyman caught up with me. In answer to my question, he replied that he was a schema monk[7] and lived in a monastery located about six miles off the main road. He invited me to come with him for a visit. "We take in pilgrims," he said, "and we offer them rest and food in the guesthouse, along with other devout people."[8]

I was reluctant to go with him, so I replied, "My peace of mind does not depend on finding shelter, but rather on obtaining spiritual guidance. I do not need food, for my knapsack is filled with dried bread."

The monk asked, "What sort of guidance do you seek, and what is it that you don't understand? Come, dear brother, and visit with us. We have experienced *startsi*[9] who can nourish you spiritually and set you on the path of truth, in the light of God's Word and the teachings of the Fathers."[10]

"Well, you see, Father, about a year ago, while at Liturgy,[11] I heard the words of the Apostle, exhorting us to 'pray without ceasing.' Unable to understand this, I began to read the Bible. There, in several different places, I also encountered this same divine instruction: that we must pray unceasingly, always and in all places, not only while occupied with any kind of activity, not only when we are awake, but even while we sleep. 'I sleep but my heart is awake.'[12] This surprised me, and I found myself unable to understand how this could be done and by what means it could be achieved. A burning desire and curiosity were aroused in me, and my thoughts dwelt on it day and night. So I began to visit many different churches and to listen to sermons that spoke about prayer. Yet, no matter how many sermons I heard, not one of them provided me with an explanation of how to pray unceasingly. They spoke only of how to prepare oneself for praying, of the fruits of prayer, and so forth; but they did not teach how one is to pray without ceasing and what the nature of this sort of prayer is. I frequently read the Bible to verify

of the New Testament, and the celebration of the Eucharist and distri-
bution of Communion among the faithful. Though structured somewhat like the Roman Catholic Mass, which is its Western equivalent, it
is entirely chanted or sung. Its celebration usually takes around two
hours, and most congregants remain standing throughout the service.

12 Song of Songs 5:2.

Pilgrims saying their prayers along the highway

what I heard, but I have not yet found the knowledge I seek. I am not at peace with myself and am still quite puzzled by all this."

The *starets* made the sign of the cross over himself and began to speak: "Thank God, beloved brother, for having awakened in you this irresistible longing to acquire unceasing interior prayer. You must recognize this as the calling of God. Be at peace, and rest assured that until now you have been tested in the cooperation of your will with God's calling and have been granted to understand that neither the wisdom of this world nor mere superficial curiosity can attain to the divine illumination of unceasing interior prayer. On the contrary, it is the humble, simple heart that attains to such prayer, through poverty of the spirit and a living experience of it. So it is not at all surprising that you heard nothing about the very essence of prayer nor acquired any knowledge on how to achieve its unceasing activity.

"To tell the truth, although much has been preached on prayer and written about it by various writers, they are better equipped to preach about the elements that constitute prayer than they are about its very essence, because their thoughts are based mostly on speculation and the deliberations of natural reason, rather than on living experience of it. One will offer an exceptional discourse on the necessity of prayer, another on its power and benefits. Yet a third will discuss the means to attaining to perfect prayer: the necessity of applied effort, attentiveness, warmth of heart, purity of thought, reconciliation with one's enemies, humility, contrition, and so on. But what about prayer itself, and how to learn to pray? To these, the most essential and necessary questions of all, very rarely does one obtain any substantial answers from present-day preachers. Such questions are far more difficult for the understanding to grasp than are all those arguments of theirs that I just mentioned, for they require a mystical insight that goes above and beyond mere academic knowledge. And what is even more pathetic is

A rural Russian church

13 1 Timothy 2:1.

14 Romans 8:28.

15 St. Isaac of Syria (late seventh century): Bishop of Nineveh; who, like a number of important early Christian writers on prayer, wrote in the now-extinct Syriac language.

that the vain, natural wisdom of this world compels one to judge the Divine according to human standards. Many people treat prayer in an inverted way, thinking that it is one's efforts and the preparatory steps that give rise to prayer, rather than the prayer itself giving birth to good works and all the virtues. In this case, they mistakenly see the fruits and resulting benefits of prayer as the means to its end, thereby denigrating the very power of prayer.

"All this stands in direct contradiction to Holy Scripture, for the Apostle Paul teaches us the following about prayer: 'I urge therefore that first of all supplications . . . be made. . . .'[13] Here we see that the Apostle's first emphasis is on the preeminence of the activity of prayer: 'I urge therefore that first of all supplications . . . be made. . . .' Many good works are required of a Christian, but it is prayer that must come first and foremost, for without prayer no other good work can be performed and one cannot find the way to the Lord. Truth cannot be acquired, the flesh with its passions and lusts cannot be crucified, the heart cannot be filled with the light of Christ and united with Him unless these are preceded by frequent prayer. I say frequent, because the proper way to pray and to attain to perfect prayer lies beyond our abilities. The Apostle Paul says, 'For we do not know how to pray as we ought.'[14] Consequently, the frequency and regularity of prayer are the only things that lie within our abilities, as the means of attaining to pure prayer, which is the mother of all spiritual blessings. 'Acquire the mother and she will bear you children,' says St. Isaac of Syria.[15] First learn to pray, and then you will easily perform all good works. This is not obvious to those who lack a living experience of prayer and the knowledge of the mystical teachings of the Fathers, so they say very little about it."

So engrossed were we in this conversation that without realizing it we had almost reached the monastery. Not wanting to lose touch with this wise starets, and eager to obtain what I desired from him, I quickly

16 *Philokalia* is the original Greek title of the work, meaning "Love of the Beautiful." The great classic of Orthodox teaching on prayer, it is an anthology of teachings by various writers from the fourth to fifteenth centuries, compiled by Saints Nicodemos of the Holy Mountain (see page 62) and Macarius Notaras, and first published in 1782. The starets would likely have had a copy of the Russian translation published by Bishop Theophan the Recluse between 1876 and 1890, and entitled in Russian *Dobrotolubye*, or "Love of the Good." It is available today in English translation in four volumes (with a fifth in process): *The Philokalia: The Complete Text*, translated from the Greek by G. E. H. Palmer, Philip Sherrard, and Kallistos Ware (London: Faber & Faber, 1979–1998). An excellent selection from the *Philokalia* focusing on teachings of the Jesus prayer is *Writings from the Philokalia on the Prayer of the Heart*, translated from the Russian by E. Kadloubovsky and G. E. H. Palmer (London: Faber & Faber, 1992).

said, "Would you be so kind, honorable Father, to explain to me the meaning of unceasing interior prayer and how one can learn it? I can see that you have experience of it and know it well."

The starets lovingly acknowledged my request and invited me to come with him. "Come inside with me now, and I will give you a book of the writings of the Fathers from which, with God's help, you will be able to learn and understand about prayer, clearly and in detail." We entered his cell, and the starets said to me: "The unceasing interior prayer of Jesus is the uninterrupted, continual calling upon the divine Name of Jesus Christ, with the lips, the mind, and the heart, while calling to mind His constant presence and beseeching His mercy, during any activity with which one may be occupied, in all places, at all times, and even while sleeping. The words of this prayer are as follows: 'Lord Jesus Christ, have mercy on me!' If one makes a habit of this supplication, he will experience great comfort and a need to repeat this prayer unceasingly, so that eventually he will not be able to live without it, and the prayer will flow from him of its own accord.

"Now is it clear to you what unceasing prayer is?"

"Very clear, my Father! For God's sake, teach me how to acquire it," I cried out with joy.

"We can read about how to learn the prayer in this book, whose title is the *Philokalia*.[16] It contains the complete and detailed teaching on unceasing interior prayer, as set forth by twenty-five holy Fathers. The wisdom it contains is so exalted and beneficial that it is considered to be the foremost and primary manual of the contemplative spiritual life. The blessed Nikifor said that 'without struggle and sweat does it bring one to salvation.'"

"Can it be that the *Philokalia* is more exalted and holier than the Bible?" I asked.

"No, it is not more exalted or holier than the Bible, but it contains

17 St. Symeon the New Theologian (949–1022): Spiritual writer and monk of Constantinople, at the monasteries of Studios and St. Mamas, where he eventually became abbot. He was a formative influence on hesychasm, "quietude," another term for the practice of the Jesus prayer. St. Symeon's works available in English are *Symeon the New Theologian: The Discourses*, translated by C. J. de Catanzaro (Mahwah, N.J.: Paulist Press, 1980) and *On the Mystical Life: The Ethical Discourses on Virtue and Christian Life* (Crestwood, N.Y.: St. Vladimir's Seminary Press, 1996).

18 St. Gregory of Sinai (died 1360): A monk ordained in Sinai (hence his name) who learned interior prayer on Mount Athos (see page 62) and went on to teach it throughout the region. Known especially for his teachings on spiritual sobriety—the ability to remain firm in prayer without being led astray by emotional states.

19 Blessed Callistus and Ignatius of Xanthopoulos (mid-fourteenth century) were close friends and coteachers of prayer who received their monastic training on Mount Athos (see page 62), and were students of St. Gregory of Sinai. Callistus became Patriarch of Constantinople about 1360. They were coauthors of the book *Directions to Hesychasts in a Hundred Chapters*, which is found in its entirety in the *Philokalia*.

20 Matins: The morning church service of the daily monastic cycle of services, performed sometime between three A.M. and nine. In Russia it was also often celebrated the night before a feast day, or on Saturday nights, a practice that continues to this day.

enlightened explanations of what is mystically contained in the Bible, and it is so lofty that it is not easily comprehended by our shortsighted intellects. Let me give you an illustration. The sun is the greatest, the most resplendent and magnificent source of light, but you cannot contemplate or examine it with the simple naked eye. You would need to use a special viewing lens, which, though a million times smaller and dimmer than the sun, would enable you to study this magnificent source of all light and to endure and delight in its fiery rays. Thus the Holy Scriptures are like a brilliant sun, for which the *Philokalia* is the lens needed in order to view it.

"Look, I will read to you about how to learn unceasing interior prayer." The starets opened the *Philokalia*. He chose a passage from St. Symeon the New Theologian[17] and began to read: "'Find a quiet place to sit alone and in silence; bow your head and shut your eyes. Breathe softly, look with your mind into your heart; recollect your mind—that is, all its thoughts—and bring them down from your mind into your heart. As you breathe, repeat: "Lord Jesus Christ, have mercy on me," either quietly with your lips, or only in your mind. Make an effort to banish all thoughts; be calm and patient, and repeat this exercise frequently.'"

The starets then explained all this to me and illustrated it with examples, and we read more from the *Philokalia*: passages from St. Gregory of Sinai[18] and from the blessed Callistus and Ignatius.[19] After reading all this to me, the starets further explained it to me in his own words. I was fascinated and listened attentively to every word he said, absorbing it with my mind in as much detail as I was capable. Thus we spent the entire night, without sleeping at all, and then went off to the matins service.[20]

As we parted, the starets blessed me and said that while learning the prayer, I should come to see him and reveal and confess all to him

21 "Standing in church": Traditionally, Orthodox churches contain no pews or other seating other than a few benches for the aged and infirm. This practice is today relaxed, particularly in churches in North America. But in the pilgrim's time there would have been no seating. He, and everyone else, would be expected to stand throughout the entire service.

❖ Hesychasm: from the Greek *hesychia*, "quietness." Though this word is not used in *The Way of a Pilgrim*, it is the term synonymous with the practice of the Jesus prayer that the pilgrim learns and comes to exemplify, and of which the *Philokalia* is the central text.

Though hesychasm and the use of short, repetitive prayers such as the Jesus prayer are ancient practices with many antecedents in the early Fathers, hesychasm is particularly associated with the figure of St. Gregory Palamas (1296–1359), onetime monk of Mount Athos (see page 62) and the bishop of the city of Thessalonika (present-day Thessaloniki, Greece), who struggled to present its theological justification against its detractors, thus ensuring its central place in Orthodox spirituality to this day. Palamas' works such as *Triads in Defense of the Holy Hesychasts* argue that the goal of contemplative prayer is knowledge of God—and that God truly communicates himself to humans in prayer. His opponents' claim was that God was ultimately unknowable. He was vindicated by Church councils of Constantinople in 1347 and 1351.

A practitioner of hesychasm, like the pilgrim, is called a *hesychast*.

honestly and openly, for it is difficult and futile to live in an inner spiritual life properly without the guidance of a spiritual director.

Standing in church,[21] I experienced a burning zeal within me to learn unceasing interior prayer as diligently as possible, and I asked God to help me in this effort. Then the thought arose: how will I be able to visit the starets for counsel and confession, when the monastery guesthouse has a three-day limit for visitors and there are no other residences near the monastery? Finally I happened to hear that there was a village a little over three miles away. I went there in search of a place to stay and was overjoyed that God had led me to find such a place. A peasant hired me to guard his kitchen garden for the entire summer, in exchange for which he allowed me to live by myself in a hut near the garden. Thank God I had found a peaceful place to stay! So I settled into my dwelling and began to learn interior prayer according to the way I had been taught, and I visited the starets from time to time.

For a week, in the seclusion of the garden, I worked diligently on learning unceasing prayer, and I did what the starets had taught me. At first it seemed as if things were moving along. Then a great inner heaviness, laziness, boredom, and drowsiness began to overcome me, while a mass of thoughts clouded my mind. Filled with grief, I went to see the starets and explained my problems to him. He greeted me kindly and said, "That, my beloved brother, is the kingdom of darkness waging war against you. There is nothing more dreadful for this darkness than the prayer of the heart, so it will try anything to thwart your efforts in learning to pray. Come to think of it, even the enemy can act only by God's will and permission, and only for as long as it may be necessary for us. It appears that your humility still needs to be tested. Consequently, it is too soon for you to be attempting to enter into your deepest heart with such unrestrained zeal, lest you succumb to spiritual avarice. I will read to you what the *Philokalia* says about this."

22 Blessed Nicephorus the Solitary (died 1340): A monk of Mount Athos and one of the teachers of St. Gregory Palamas (see page 18). The starets reads from his work "A Most Profitable Discourse on Sobriety and the Guarding of the Heart," which combines Nicephorus' own teaching on the prayer along with passages from various other Fathers' works.

23 Chotki: Prayer rope (*komvoskoini* in Greek). A woolen string of knots, usually black, usually consisting of 100 knots, each tied in a complicated and symbolic way, and used by Orthodox Christians in counting prayers—comparable to Roman Catholic rosary beads, Muslim *tasbih*, or Buddhist and Hindu *malas*. A cross is usually woven into the end, with a tassel said to be for wiping away tears. Other common "sizes" are 33-, 300-, and 500-knot. Chotki are also made from beads of various kinds, leather, seeds, or shells.

A chotki, or prayer rope

He found a passage from the teaching of Blessed Nicephorus the Solitary[22] and began to read: "'If, after a few attempts, you are unable to enter into the place of the heart, as you were taught to do, then do what I tell you and, with God's help, you will find what you seek. You know that each person has a larynx through which he exercises his faculty of speech. Banishing all thoughts (you can do this, if you want to), exercise this faculty and continually repeat the following: "Lord Jesus Christ, have mercy on me!" Compel yourself always to repeat this. Should you do this for some period of time, then assuredly this exercise will open the doors of your heart. Experience has proved this.'

"So this is what the holy Fathers prescribe in such cases," said the starets. "Therefore, you must accept this teaching now with complete trust, and repeat the Jesus prayer as often as possible. Take this *chotki*[23] and use it while you repeat the prayer, at least three thousand times a day to begin with. Whether you are standing, sitting, walking, or lying down, continue to repeat: 'Lord Jesus Christ, have mercy on me!' Do not be loud or rush the prayer, but without fail repeat it three thousand times each day, neither increasing nor decreasing this number on your own. Through this exercise God will help you to attain the unceasing prayer of the heart."

I joyfully accepted his instructions, went home, and began to carry out the bidding of the starets faithfully and accurately. For two days I experienced some difficulty, but then the exercise became so easy and so desirable that if I stopped, I experienced a kind of compelling need to start reciting the prayer again. Soon I was praying it with comfort and ease, without any of the effort that I had to exert at first.

I related this to the starets, who instructed me to increase the number of repetitions to six thousand times a day. "Be calm, and just try to repeat the prayer as faithfully as you can for the number of times I have assigned to you. God will bestow His mercy on you."

ΦΙΛΟΚΑΛΙΑ

ΤΩΝ ΙΕΡΩΝ

ΝΗΠΤΙΚΩΝ·

ΣΥΝΕΡΑΝΙΣΘΕΙΣΑ

ΠΑΡΑ ΤΩΝ ΑΓΙΩΝ ΚΑΙ ΘΕΟΦΟΡΩΝ

ΠΑΤΕΡΩΝ ΗΜΩΝ

ΕΝ ᾙ,

*Διὰ τῆς κατὰ τὴν Πρᾶξιν καὶ Θεωρίαν Ἠθικῆς Φιλο-
σοφίας ὁ νῦς καθαίρεται, φωτίζεται, καὶ τελειῦται·*

ΕΠΙΜΕΛΕΙΑ ΜΕΝ ΟΤΙ ΠΛΕΙΣΤῌ ΔΙΟΡΘΩΘΕΙΣΑ·

ΝΤΝ ΔΕ ΠΡΩΤΟΝ ΤΥΠΟΙΣ ΕΚΔΟΘΕΙΣΑ

ΔΙΑ ΔΑΠΑΝΗΣ

ΤΟΥ ΤΙΜΙΩΤΑΤΟΥ, ΚΑΙ ΘΕΟΣΕΒΕΣΤΑΤΟΥ ΚΥΡΙΟΥ

ΙΩΑΝΝΟΥ ΜΑΥΡΟΓΟΡΔΑΤΟΥ

ΕΙΣ ΚΟΙΝΗΝ ΤΩΝ ΟΡΘΟΔΟΞΩΝ ΩΦΕΛΕΙΑΝ.

αψπβ'. ΕΝΕΤΙΗΣΙΝ, 1782.

ΠΑΡΑ ΑΝΤΩΝΙΩ ΤΩ ΒΟΡΤΟΛΙ.

CON LICENZA DE'SUPERIORI, E PRIVILEGIO.

Title page of the original Greek Philokalia, 1782

For an entire week, in the solitude of my hut, I repeated the Jesus prayer six thousand times a day. I was not anxious about anything and paid no heed to any thoughts, no matter how strongly they assailed me. I concentrated only on precisely carrying out the starets's instructions. And do you know what happened? I became so accustomed to the prayer that when I stopped praying, even for a brief time, I felt as though something were missing, as if I had lost something. When I began to pray again, I was immediately filled with an inner lightness and joy. If I happened to meet someone, I no longer felt any desire to speak with him. I longed only for solitude, to be alone with my prayer. Thus it was that within a week I had become accustomed to this prayer.

After ten days of not seeing me, the starets himself came to visit me, and I described my inner state to him. He listened and said, "Now that you have become accustomed to the prayer, take care to preserve and strengthen this habit. Do not pass your time in vain and, with God's help, resolve to repeat the prayer, without fail, twelve thousand times a day. Remain in solitude, rise earlier in the morning, retire later at night, and come to me for counsel every two weeks."

I began to carry out the starets's instructions. By late evening of the first day, I had barely managed to complete the rule of twelve thousand repetitions of the prayer. On the second day, I fulfilled the rule with ease and delight. At first I was weary from repeating the prayer continuously. My tongue became numb and my jaws felt stiff, although the sensations were not unpleasant. I then felt a subtle, delicate pain in the roof of my mouth, followed by a slight pain in the thumb with which I was counting the knots of the chotki. My wrist felt inflamed, and this feeling spread up to my elbow, creating a most pleasant sensation. Moreover, all this was somehow urging and compelling me to pray more and more. Thus, for the first five days I faithfully repeated the prayer twelve thousand times a day. As this habit became stronger it also

❖   "For as the more the rain pours down upon the earth, the more it softens the earth; so too the holy name of Christ, when it is invoked by us without thoughts, the more constantly we call upon it, the more it softens the earth of our heart, and fills it with joy and delight."

—from the *Philokalia*: Heyschius of Jerusalem, *To Theodulus*, 41

A Russian monk

became more enjoyable, and I found myself more willing to practice it.

Early one morning somehow the prayer awakened me. I began to recite my morning prayers, but my tongue resisted saying them, while all my desire seemed to be striving, as if with a mind of its own, toward reciting the Jesus prayer. As soon as I began to repeat it, I was filled with such lightness and joy that it felt as if my tongue and mouth spoke the words of their own accord, without any effort on my part! I spent the entire day wrapped up in such joy and somehow detached from everything else—almost as though I were on another planet. By early evening I had easily completed the twelve thousand repetitions of the prayer. I had a strong desire to continue praying, but I dared not exceed the rule given to me by the starets. In the days that followed, I continued to call on the name of Jesus Christ with such ease and feeling so drawn to it.

Then I visited the starets and honestly recounted all this to him in detail. He listened and said, "Thank God that the ease and desire for prayer have been manifested in you. This is the natural result of frequent practice and great effort. It is similar to a piece of equipment that can operate for a long time on its own, once its main drive has been activated; but in order for it to continue operating, the drive must be oiled and regularly reactivated. Now do you see with what superior abilities God, in his love for us, has endowed even the most sensual human nature, and what feelings can be experienced even outside a state of grace, even by a sinful soul with unclean passions, as you yourself have already experienced? Yet how magnificent, how delightful and enjoyable it is when the Lord bestows the gift of unceasing self-acting prayer and purifies the soul of its passions! This state is indescribable, and the revelation of the mystery of such prayer is a foretaste of heavenly bliss on earth. This is granted to those who seek the Lord in the simplicity of a heart filled with love! I now give you leave to repeat the prayer as much as you desire and as frequently as possible. Strive to devote every

24 The starets: The nineteenth century in Russia was in many ways the golden age of the monastic elder, or starets. Monastic life had been constricted under government control during most of the eighteenth century, beginning with the accession of Peter the Great in 1721. The result was a monastic institution in need of spiritual revival. That revival came toward the end of the reign of Catherine II ("the Great") in 1796, largely through the influence of the monk Paissy Velichkovsky (1722–1794).

Velichovsky left his home in the Ukraine as a young man in search of genuine spirituality (not having found it in the monasteries of his day), traveling to Mount Athos (see page 62), where he spent several years, translating numerous Greek texts on prayer into Russian. He set out again for Russia, but got only as far as the mountains of Wallachia (in present-day Romania), where he settled, spending the rest of his life as abbot and spiritual director of several monasteries, both men's and women's. Though he never made it back to his homeland, his translations, along with his influence in general, contributed to the monastic revival of the 1800s.

At the time of the pilgrim's travels, that revival was in full swing, and many monasteries had one or more charismatic startsi, to whom monks and laypeople alike flocked for advice. Some monasteries were famous for an entire succession of influential elders, particularly the great foundation of Optina, whose starets Amvrossy is believed to have been the model for Father Zossima in Fyodor Dostoyevsky's novel *The Brothers Karamazov*.

waking moment to prayer. Do not count the number of repetitions any more, but call on the name of Jesus Christ, submitting yourself humbly to the will of God and awaiting His help. I believe that He will not abandon you and will set you on the right path."

Under the guidance of my starets, I spent the entire summer continuously repeating the Jesus prayer. I was very much at peace and often even dreamed that I was saying the prayer. If I happened to meet people during the day, each of them without exception seemed very dear to me, as if they were family, though otherwise I did not concern myself with them much. All thoughts seemed to vanish on their own, and I thought of nothing else but the prayer. My mind was recollected and attentive to it, while at times, and of its own accord, my heart would feel a warmth and a sort of pleasure. When I happened to go to church, the long monastic service seemed short and was no longer as tiring. My solitary hut seemed like a splendid palace, and I didn't know how to thank God for sending such a sinner as myself to a starets[24] and guide to salvation.

I was not able to enjoy for much longer the wise counsel of my kind, divinely inspired starets, however, for at the end of that summer he died. As I tearfully parted with him I thanked him for the fatherly counsel he had given to me and begged him to give me, for a blessing and keepsake, the chotki he always used to pray with. And so I was left alone. The summer finally drew to an end, the kitchen garden was cleared, and I was left with nowhere to live. The peasant released me from my job, paying me two rubles for my work, and filled my knapsack with dried bread for my journey. Once again I set off wandering through different places, but now my travels were free of worry. Calling on the name of Jesus Christ now filled my days with joy. Each person I encountered seemed dearer to me, as if all were filled with love for me.

At one point I began to wonder what to do with the wages I had

25 Sign of the cross: The sign of the cross is employed with much greater frequency among Orthodox Christians in general than it is among Roman Catholics or Anglicans, and this was especially true in Russia, where one would see the action repeated countless times in a day in a variety of situations. The pilgrim's making the sign of the cross before setting out to buy a copy of the *Philokalia* is an action that would be typical of a pious person undertaking any activity upon which he sought God's blessing.

In religious context, the sign of the cross is made not only upon entering and leaving the church, but many times throughout the service, as well. The sign is made somewhat differently than in the Western Church: thumb, index finger, and middle finger of the right hand are pressed together, while the other two fingers are pressed into the palm. The three fingers are touched to the forehead, stomach, right shoulder, then left shoulder, usually with a bow.

26 Starosta: A layperson in charge of taking care of a church. Sometimes also the head man of a village community.

earned for guarding the kitchen garden. What did I need money for? "Aha!" I thought, "I've got it! The starets is no longer around and there is no one to teach me. So I'll buy myself a copy of the *Philokalia* and continue learning about interior prayer." I made the sign of the cross[25] and went on walking and praying. When I came to a provincial town, I searched through the shops for a copy of the *Philokalia*. I found one, but they were asking three rubles for it, and I had only two! After bargaining a long time, the shopkeeper still refused to lower the price. Finally he said, "Go to that church over there and ask the *starosta*.[26] He has an old copy of this book; maybe he'll sell it to you for two rubles." I went there and was actually able to buy the *Philokalia* for two rubles! It was an old and worn copy, but I was thrilled to have it. I managed to mend it somewhat, using a piece of cloth, and I placed it in my knapsack together with my Bible.

I set out again, continuously praying the Jesus prayer, which had become more precious and sweeter to me than anything else in the world. There were days when I covered forty-seven miles or more, and I didn't even feel the effort of walking. The prayer alone filled my consciousness. When it was bitterly cold, I would pray more fervently, and soon I would feel warm all over. If hunger threatened to overcome me, I would call upon the name of Jesus Christ with renewed vigor, and soon my hunger was forgotten. If I felt ill and pain racked my back and legs, I would give myself over to the prayer and would soon be immune to the pain. If someone offended me, I needed only to remember the sweetness of the Jesus prayer, and all hurt and anger vanished; all was forgotten. It was as if I'd become a half-wit, for I had no cares about anything. Nothing interested me. I cared nothing for the vain concerns of this world and longed only for solitude. I was now accustomed to desiring only one thing: to pray unceasingly, for that was what filled me with joy. God alone knows what was happening to me! But of course, all these

27 The practice of the Jesus prayer is thought to fall into three basic "parts": (1) first, the prayer is repeated over and over again with the lips, as a means of forming the habit of it in the body; (2) next, it is brought into the mind, with an effort made on learning concentration and the ability to send away competing thoughts; and (3) then the prayer enters the heart, living itself in the hesychast with every heartbeat.

Paissy Velichkovsky

were feelings—or, as my late starets would say, a natural habit. However, in my unworthiness and foolishness, I dared not venture yet to learn and aspire to the prayer of the inner heart.[27] I awaited the fulfillment of God's will, setting my hopes on the prayers of my departed starets. And so, though I had not yet achieved the unceasing self-acting prayer of the heart, still I thanked God! For now I understood clearly the meaning of the Apostle's words that I had heard: "Pray without ceasing!"

Second
Narrative

1 "For a long time I wandered": A life of pilgrimage such as was under-
taken by the narrator was a fairly common practice in Russia from
medieval times on. Pilgrims *(stranniki)* adopted a life of wandering
among the monasteries and shrines and often spent their entire lives in
such traveling. They were a regular feature of the Russian countryside.

2 St. Innocent of Irkutsk (1680–1731) was a missionary to Siberia in
the days when Russia's vast Asian region was still very much on the
frontier. His tomb was a popular site of pilgrimage.

Irkutsk sits on the western shore of Lake Baikal, near the border of
Mongolia, not far from China. A journey on foot to Irkutsk is a major
undertaking—the pilgrim's journey from European Russia would have
been at least two thousand miles long.

For a long time I wandered around through different places accompanied by the Jesus prayer, which encouraged and comforted me wherever I went, no matter what or whom I encountered.[1] Finally it occurred to me that it might be preferable for me to settle down somewhere for a while, in order to find time and solitude for studying the *Philokalia*. Although I had managed to read bits of it whenever I stopped for the night or for a moment of rest, I longed to immerse myself in it without interruption and, with faith, to learn from it the true way to salvation through the prayer of the heart.

However, in spite of my wish and because of the disability I'd had in my left arm from the time I was a child, I was unable find work. Since I was unable to manage the upkeep of a permanent residence, I headed for Siberia to visit the grave of St. Innocent of Irkutsk.[2] It seemed to me that the Siberian forests and steppes would allow for quieter and more peaceful traveling and would make it easier for me to pray and read. So I set out, repeating the prayer continuously with my lips.

Finally, after a short time, I felt that the prayer began to move of its own accord from my lips into my heart. That is to say, it seemed as if my heart, while beating naturally, somehow began to repeat within itself the words of the prayer in rhythm with its natural beating: (1) Lord . . . (2) Jesus . . . (3) Christ . . . and so on. I then stopped reciting the words of the prayer with my lips and began to listen attentively to the words of my heart, remembering what my starets had said about how pleasant this would be. Then I began to experience a delicate soreness in

❖ "There are degrees of the action of the prayer of Jesus. At first it acts only on the mind, leading it to a state of calm and attention. Afterwards it begins to penetrate to the heart, arousing it from the sleep of death and making its revival known by the manifestation within it of feelings of compunction and sorrow. As it goes still deeper, it gradually begins to act upon all the members of the soul and body and to expel sin from every part, and everywhere to destroy the dominion, influence, and poison of the demons. For this reason at the first actions of the prayer of Jesus there occurs 'unutterable contrition and unspeakable pain of soul,' says St. Gregory the Sinaite."

—Ignatius Brianchaninov, *On the Prayer of Jesus,* p. 35

my heart, and my thoughts were filled with such a love for Jesus Christ that it seemed to me that if I were to see Him, I would throw myself down, embrace His feet, and never let them go, kissing them tenderly and tearfully. And I would thank Him for His love and mercy in granting such consolation through His name to His unworthy and sinful creature!

Then a wholesome warmth began to fill my heart, and it seemed to spread throughout my chest. This warmth especially moved me to an attentive reading of the *Philokalia*, both to verify the feelings I had experienced and to further my knowledge of the prayer of the heart. I was afraid that without this verification I might fall into delusion or mistake natural activity for the action of grace and succumb to the pride, which the starets had spoken of, in having attained so quickly to this prayer.

So I took to walking mostly at night and spent my days sitting in the forest, under the trees, reading the *Philokalia*. Ah, how much new knowledge, how much wisdom that I had never yet possessed, was revealed to me in this book! As I began to put it into practice I experienced a sweetness I could not have even imagined before. Although it is true that some of the passages I read were not immediately understandable to my foolish mind, the effects of the prayer of the heart clarified whatever I failed to understand. At times my starets came to me in my dreams and explained so much to me. Above all else, he inclined my ignorant soul toward humility. For more than two months that summer, I basked in this blissful state while I walked, keeping to the forests and back roads. When I came to a village I would ask for dry bread to fill my knapsack, and for a handful of salt. Then I would fill my bark jar with water, and on I would go for almost another seventy miles.

❖

ДОБРОТОЛЮБІЕ

ВЪ РУССКОМЪ ПЕРЕВОДѢ,

ДОПОЛНЕННОЕ.

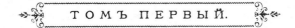

ТОМЪ ПЕРВЫЙ.

ИЗДАНІЕ ЧЕТВЕРТОЕ.

Иждивеніемъ Русскаго на Аѳонѣ Пантелеимонова монастыря.

МОСКВА.
Типо-Литографія И. Ефимова. Большая Якиманка, собственный домъ.
1905.

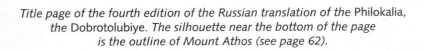

Title page of the fourth edition of the Russian translation of the Philokalia,
the Dobrotolubiye. *The silhouette near the bottom of the page
is the outline of Mount Athos (see page 62).*

For a long time I walked through forests and only rarely came across a small village. Sometimes I would spend an entire day sitting in the forest, going very carefully over the *Philokalia* and learning many wonderful things from it. My heart burned with a desire for union with God through interior prayer, which I strove to attain to under the guidance and verification of the *Philokalia*. Yet, I also grieved that I had not yet found a permanent residence where I could spend all my time reading in peace.

During this time I also read my Bible and felt that I was beginning to understand it better than I had before, when so much was still unclear and puzzling to me. How right the Fathers are when they say the *Philokalia* is the key to unlocking the mysteries of Holy Scripture. With its guidance, I began to understand parts of the hidden meaning of the Word of God. The meanings of such statements as "the inner hidden man of the heart," "true prayer," "worshiping in the spirit," "the Kingdom of Heaven is within us," "the intercession of the Holy Spirit with unutterable groanings," "abide in me," "give me your heart," "to put on Christ," the "betrothal of the Spirit to our hearts," calling from one's heart "Abba, Father!" and so on were now being revealed to me. As I began to pray now with my heart, everything around me was delightfully transformed: the trees, the grass, the birds, the ground, the air, the light—all seemed to proclaim that they exist for the sake of man and bear witness to the love of God for man. All creation prays to God and sings His praises. From this I understood what the *Philokalia* calls a "knowledge of the language of all creation," and I saw how it is possible for us to communicate with all of God's creatures.

I traveled this way for a long time until, finally, I found myself in a place so little inhabited that for three days I did not see a single village. I had eaten all my dried bread, and I worried that I might die of hunger. Yet, as soon as I began to pray, all despair would vanish. I gave myself

❖ "At first the practice of the prayer of Jesus appears to be extraordinarily dry and seems to promise no fruit. As the mind strives to unite with the heart, it meets first with impenetrable darkness and gloom, hardness and deadness of the heart, which is not quickly aroused to sympathy with the mind. This should not cause despondency and cowardice; it is mentioned here since to be forewarned is to be forearmed. The patient and diligent worker will not fail to be satisfied and consoled; he will rejoice at an infinite abundance of spiritual fruits such as he can form no conception of in his carnal and natural state."

—Ignatius Brianchaninov, *On the Prayer of Jesus*, p. 35

3   Bread and salt: Russian symbols of hospitality, traditionally offered to guests upon their arrival.

over entirely to the will of God and was filled with joy and peace. As I walked along part of the road that ran next to the forest I saw a mongrel dog come running out of the trees ahead of me. It approached when I called to it and began to play with me affectionately. I was overjoyed and thought to myself, "Now there's God's mercy for you! There must be a flock grazing in this forest, and of course this well-trained dog belongs to the shepherd; or perhaps there is a hunter nearby. Whatever the case, at least I'll be able to beg for some bread from him—I haven't eaten in twenty-four hours. Or I can at least ask him where the nearest village is."

The dog had been jumping around me and, when it realized I had nothing to give it, ran off into the forest down the same narrow path by which it had come out. I followed it, and about five hundred yards later I saw that the dog had run into a hole between some trees, from which it kept looking out and barking.

At that very moment, a thin, pale, middle-aged peasant emerged from behind a tree. He asked me how I had come to be there, and I asked him the same. We struck up a friendly conversation, and he invited me into his hut. He told me that he was a forester and was guarding this part of the woods, which had been sold to be felled for lumber. He offered me bread and salt,[3] and we began to talk. "I envy you," I said "because you live in such comfortable solitude, so far removed from everyone, while I wander from place to place, mixing with all sorts of people."

"If you'd like to," he said, "perhaps you could live here too. There's an old mud hut not far from here that belonged to the previous watchman. It's run down, of course, but it's livable in the summer. You have a passport, and we'll have enough bread to eat; they supply me with it weekly from the village. There's a stream here that never dries up. For ten years now, my brother, I myself have eaten nothing but bread. I never drink anything but water. There is one thing, however: in the

❖ "The *Philokalia* is an itinerary through the labyrinth of time, a silent way of love and gnosis through the deserts and emptinesses of life, especially of modern life, a vivifying and fadeless presence. It is an active force revealing a spiritual path and inducing man to follow it. It is a summons to him to overcome his ignorance, to uncover the knowledge that lies within, to rid himself of illusion, and to be receptive to the grace of the Holy Spirit who teaches all things and brings all things to remembrance."

—G. E. H. Palmer, Philip Sherrard, Archimandrite Kallistos Ware, from the introduction to *The Philokalia: The Complete Text,* volume one

fall, when the peasants finish working on the land, about two hundred of them will gather here to chop down all the trees in this forest. Then my job here will be over, and you won't be allowed to remain either."

When I heard all this, I was so overjoyed that I could have thrown myself at his feet. I knew not how to thank God for showing me such mercy. What I had desired and longed for was now being given to me unexpectedly. There were still more than four months left until late fall. Here I could find the peace and solitude that I needed to immerse myself in reading the *Philokalia* and in learning how to attain to the unceasing prayer of the heart. So I settled down joyfully in the hut he pointed out to me, for whatever time had been given me to live there. I talked some more with this simple brother who had offered me shelter, and he told me about his life and his thoughts on it.

"In my village," he said, "I had a good position; I dyed cotton and linen for a living. I led a prosperous life, though not a sinless one. I sometimes cheated in business and took false oaths; I cursed, drank liquor, and got into fights. There was an old deacon in our village who had an extremely old book about the Last Judgment. He would visit the faithful and read to them from it, for which they gave him money. And he also visited me. Give him about ten kopecks, and he could read into the night till the cock crowed. So I'd sit and work, listening to him read about the torments that await us in hell, how the living would be transformed and the dead would be resurrected, how God would come down to judge us, how the angels would sound their trumpets, of the fire and brimstone, and how the worm would devour the sinners. One time, as I listened to all this, I got scared and thought to myself, 'There's no way I'll avoid that torment! Maybe it's time I started saving my soul— maybe I could even pray my sins away.' I thought about this for a long time and decided to give up my business. Since I had no family ties, I sold my house and became a forester in exchange for being provided with

4 Prostrations: These deep bows, in which the worshiper kneels and touches the head to the floor, are a common practice of Orthodox piety, performed frequently in religious services by individuals and by the entire congregation, particularly during the period of Lent. They are also done—as the woodsman does—privately as a form of prayer, and as a way of expressing repentance and humility. Pious Russians might do as many as a hundred prostrations or more daily in their rule of private prayer.

5 Iron chains: An extreme but not unheard-of method of asceticism intended to bring the body and the passions under control. They usually consisted of an inscribed heavy iron cross attached to chains that were worn over the shoulders next to the skin.

bread, clothing, and candles for my prayers, by the village council.

"So I've lived here for more than ten years. I eat once a day, only bread and water. I get up each day at daybreak and say my prayers and do my prostrations[4] until dawn, burning seven candles in front of the icons. During the day, when I make my rounds of the forest, I wear iron chains weighing seventy-two pounds next to my skin.[5] I don't curse any more, or drink liquor, or get into any fights, and I've never been with women my entire life.

"At first I preferred this kind of life, but lately I find myself constantly attacked by thoughts. God knows if sins can really be prayed away. And it is a hard life, you know. And then, is it really true what that book says—that dead men will be resurrected? Someone who died a hundred years ago or more—why, there's not even a speck of dust left of him. For that matter, who really knows if there will even be a hell— right? Why, no one has ever come back from the dead! It seems to me that once a person dies, he rots and vanishes without a trace. Maybe that book was written by some clergy, by some high authorities, just to scare us fools to make us more humble. Life is full of hardships as it is, without any consolation—and there won't be anything in the next life. So what's the point? Isn't it better to take it easy, at least in this life, and to enjoy yourself? Such thoughts hound me," he continued, "and I wonder if I shouldn't just go back to my old job!"

Listening to him speak, I sympathized and thought to myself: they say that only the educated and the intelligent are prone to freethinking and belief in nothing. But here is one of our own—a simple peasant— and what doubts he is capable of! It appears that the powers of darkness are allowed access to everyone, and perhaps it is easier for them to attack unsophisticated people. A person must acquire wisdom and strengthen himself as much as possible with the Word of God against the spiritual enemy.

6 Hesychios: Hesychios of Jerusalem (died 432–433): A Palestinian priest, teacher, and preacher, a student of the renowned Gregory the Theologian. The pilgrim likely read from his "Texts on Sobriety and Prayer for the Saving of the Soul."

❖ "Until recently, Western theologians were highly suspicious of Athonite hesychasm and regarded it as perilous, even heretical. Deeper study and a wider acquaintance with non-Western forms of spirituality have made hesychasm seem a little less outlandish. It is no longer necessary to repeat the outraged platitudes of those who thought that the hesychasts were practicing self-hypnosis, or who believed that, at best, the monks of Athos were engaged in a kind of Western yoga.

"The prayer of Jesus, made known to Western readers by the *Tale of a Pilgrim*, surely one of the great classics in the literature of prayer, is now practiced not only by characters in Salinger's novels, but even at times by some Western monks."

—Thomas Merton, *Mystics and Zen Masters*
(New York: Farrar, Straus & Giroux, 1967) p. 180

In an effort to help and strengthen this brother's faith as much as I could, I took the *Philokalia* out of my knapsack, opened it to chapter 109, the work of the venerable Hesychios,[6] and read it to him. I then explained that to abstain from sin only out of fear of punishment is a useless and fruitless task. "The soul cannot free itself from sins of thought other than by guarding the mind and the purity of the heart, all of which is achieved by interior prayer. Moreover," I added, "the holy Fathers say that the efforts of those who strive for salvation only from a fear of hell's torments, or even solely from a desire to enter the Kingdom of God, are mercenary. They say that to fear suffering is the way of the servant, while to desire a reward in the Kingdom is the way of the mercenary. Yet, God desires that we come to Him as sons, that we be honest and delight in the redemptive union with Him in our hearts and souls—but only out of love and devotion to Him. No matter how you wear yourself out with physical labors and struggles, if you do not keep the remembrance of God in your mind and the Jesus prayer in your heart, you will never find peace from these thoughts and you will always be easily swayed by sin—even by the smallest temptations.

"Why don't you start practicing the Jesus prayer?" I said. "It would be possible and even easy for you to do with the solitude you have, and you will be able to see its benefits in no time. No godless thoughts will besiege you, and you will acquire faith and love for Jesus Christ. Then you will know how it is that the dead will be resurrected, and you will be given to understand the Last Judgment as it really will take place. Your heart will be so free of burdens and so full of joy from this prayer that you will be amazed. You'll no longer feel lonely, and you will no longer doubt the purpose of the efforts you make toward your salvation."

Then I explained to him how to begin saying the Jesus prayer and how to repeat it continuously, as the Word of God instructs us and the holy Fathers teach. He seemed willing to do this and was much calmer

❖ "I have often read the Jesus Prayer in prayer books and heard it in church, but my attention was drawn to it first some years ago in Rumania. There in a small Monastery of Smbata, tucked away at the foot of the Carpathians in the heart of the deep forest, its little white church reflected in a crystal clear mountain pond, I met a monk who practiced the 'prayer of the heart.' Profound peace and silence reigned at Smbata in those days; it was a place of rest and strength—I pray God it still is.

"I have wandered far since I last saw Smbata, and all the while the Jesus prayer lay as a precious gift buried in my heart. It remained inactive until a few years ago, when I read *The Way of a Pilgrim*. Since then I have been seeking to practice it continually. At times I lapse; nonetheless, the prayer has opened unbelievable vistas within my heart and soul."

—Mother Alexandra of Holy Transfiguration Monastery
(Princess Ileana of Romania)

7   1 Corinthinans 12:31.

8   1 Thessalonians 5:19.

now. I took leave of him then and shut myself up in the ancient mud hut that he had told me about.

My God! What joy, peace, and delight I knew the moment I set foot in that "cave"—or better yet, "tomb." It seemed to me to be the most magnificent palace, filled with every joy and consolation! I thanked God with tears of joy and thought, "Well, now, with all this peace and quiet I must seriously get back to my task, asking the Lord to guide me." So I began by reading the *Philokalia* very carefully, starting with the first chapter and going all the way to the end. It did not take too long to read it through, and I realized what wisdom, holiness, and depth it contained. Yet, it covered so many different subjects and contained so many different teachings of the holy Fathers that I was unable to understand everything or to piece together all that I wanted to learn, especially about interior prayer, so that I could draw from it the knowledge of how to attain to the unceasing self-acting prayer of the heart. I longed for this, in keeping with God's commandment and as it was spoken through His apostle: "But earnestly desire the higher gifts,"[7] and again: "Do not quench the Spirit."[8]

I thought about this for a long time. What could I do? I would start badgering the Lord with prayers; perhaps the Lord would somehow enlighten me. So I did nothing but pray continuously for the next twenty-four hours, not stopping for even a moment. My thoughts were calmed, and I fell asleep. In a dream I saw myself sitting in the cell of my departed starets. He was explaining the *Philokalia* to me, saying, "This holy book is full of great wisdom. It is a mystical treasury of the meanings of the hidden judgments of God. It is not made accessible everywhere and to everyone, but it does offer instruction according to the measure of each reader's understanding. Thus, to the wise it offers wise guidance, while to the simple-minded it yields simple guidance. That is why you simple ones should not read it section by section, in the order

9 Those wishing to read the *Philokalia* in the order indicated here by the starets should see *Writings from the Philokalia on the Prayer of the Heart*, translated from the Russian by E. Kadloubovsky and G. E. H. Palmer (London: Faber & Faber, 1979). The selections included in this volume consist of all his prescribed readings in the order recommended.

10 Nicephorus the Solitary: See page 20.

11 St. Gregory of Sinai: See page 16.

12 St. Symeon the New Theologian: See page 16.

13 Callistus and Ignatius: See page 16.

that the teachings of the different holy Fathers appear in the book.[9]

"First read the book of Nicephorus the Solitary (in part 2)[10]; then read the entire book of St. Gregory of Sinai,[11] excluding the short chapters; then read Symeon the New Theologian[12] on the three kinds of prayer, and his Discourse on Faith; and afterward read the book of Callistus and Ignatius.[13] The work of these Fathers contains the complete instruction and teaching on the interior prayer of the heart and can be understood by all.

"Then, if you should want an even clearer teaching on prayer, turn to section 4 for the summary on methods of prayer, by Callistus the most holy Patriarch of Constantinople." In my dream I held the *Philokalia* in my hands and began to look for this passage, but I could not find it right away. The starets flipped through a few pages and said, "Here it is! I will mark the place for you." He picked up a piece of charcoal from the ground and made a mark with it in the margin, next to the passage. I listened carefully to everything the starets said and tried to remember it in as much detail as I could. Since it was not yet dawn when I woke up, I lay in bed and went over every detail of my dream and everything the starets had told me. Finally I began to wonder, "God alone knows if this is really the soul of the late starets who is appearing to me in my dream, or if it is all in my mind, since I think so often about him and the *Philokalia*."

Still puzzled by all this, I got out of bed, for the light of day was dawning. And what did I see? I looked at the rock that served me as a table and saw the *Philokalia* lying there, open to the very passage that the starets had pointed out to me in the dream, with the same charcoal mark he had made in the dream, exactly as I had dreamed it—the piece of charcoal even lay next to the book! This astonished me, for I clearly remembered that the book had not been there the evening before; in fact, I had wrapped it up and placed it at the head of my bed before I

❖ "The texts in the *Philokalia* were written by and for those actively living not only within the sacramental and liturgical framework of the Orthodox Church, but also within that of the Orthodox monastic tradition. They therefore presuppose conditions of life radically different from those in which most readers of this English translation are likely to find themselves. Is this tantamount to saying that the counsels they contain can be applied only within a monastic environment? Many hesychast writers affirm that this is not the case, and St. Nikodimos himself, in his introduction to the original *Philokalia*, goes out of his way to stress that 'unceasing prayer' may or, rather, should be practiced by all. Naturally, the monastic life provides conditions, such as quietness, solitude, and regularity, indispensable for that concentration without which one cannot advance far along the spiritual path. But provided that the basic condition of active participation in the sacramental and liturgical life of the Church is fulfilled, then this path is open for all to follow, each to the best of his or her ability and whatever the circumstances under which he or she lives. Indeed, in this respect the distinction between the monastic life and life 'in the world' is but relative: every human being, by virtue of the fact that he or she is created in the image of God, is summoned to be perfect, is summoned to love God with all his or her heart, soul, and mind. In this sense, all have the same vocation and all must follow the same spiritual path."

—G. E. H. Palmer, Philip Sherrard, Archimandrite Kallistos Ware,
from the introduction to *The Philokalia: The Complete Text,* volume one

went to sleep. I was also quite sure that there had been no mark next to this particular passage. This incident finally convinced me of the reality of my dreams and that my starets of blessed memory had found favor in the eyes of God.

So I started reading the *Philokalia*, in the exact order the starets had indicated. I read it through once and then a second time, and my soul burned with a desire and eagerness to experience personally all that I had read about. The meaning of interior prayer was revealed clearly to my understanding: the way it was attained, what its fruits were, how it delights the soul and the heart, and how to discern whether this sweet delight is from God, from natural causes, or the result of delusion.

So I began first to seek the place of the heart, according to the teaching of Symeon the New Theologian. I closed my eyes and gazed mentally into my heart; I tried to visualize it in the left part of my chest cavity and carefully listened to its beating. I began doing this exercise for half an hour, several times a day. At first I saw only total darkness, but soon a picture of my heart, along with the sound of its natural beating, formed in my mind. Then I began to repeat the Jesus prayer in my heart, in steady rhythm with my breathing, as taught by St. Gregory of Sinai, Callistus, and Ignatius: namely, by concentrating my mind in the heart while visualizing it in my mind, I inhaled saying, "Lord Jesus Christ," and then exhaled saying, "Have mercy on me." At first I did this exercise for an hour or two. As I progressed I increased the time, until finally I was able to repeat the exercise for almost the entire day. Whenever fatigue, laziness, or doubt came over me, I immediately turned to reading the *Philokalia*, specifically those passages that deal with the work of the heart, and all desire and eagerness were restored.

After about three weeks I began to experience a soreness in my heart, followed by the most delightful warmth, joy, and peace. This increasingly stirred me and kindled my desire to practice the prayer

14 The supernatural "gift of tears" is frequently spoken of in Orthodox spiritual texts. Here is a passage on the topic from the *Philokalia*,
from the *Mystic Treatises* by Isaac of Nineveh:

> The fruits of the inner man begin only with the shedding of
> tears. When you reach the place of tears, then know that your
> spirit has come out from the prison of this world and has set its
> foot upon the path that leads towards the new age. Your spirit
> begins at this moment to breathe the wonderful air which is
> there, and it starts to shed tears. The moment for the birth of
> the spiritual child is now at hand, and the travail of childbirth
> becomes intense. Grace, the common mother of us all, makes
> haste to give birth mystically to the soul, God's image, bring-
> ing it forth into the light of the age to come. And when the
> time for the birth has arrived, the intellect begins to sense
> something of the things of that other world—as a faint per-
> fume, or as the breath of life which a newborn child receives
> into its bodily frame. But we are not accustomed to such an
> experience, and, finding it hard to endure, our body is sud-
> denly overcome by a weeping mingled with joy.

15 From Luke 17:20–21: "Being asked by the Pharisees when the kingdom of God was coming, he answered them, 'The kingdom of God is
not coming with signs to be observed; nor will they say, "Lo, here it is!"
or "There!" for behold, the kingdom of God is within you'" (Revised
Standard Version).

more diligently, so that I thought about nothing else and was filled with an immense joy. From then on, at times I would experience different sensations in my heart and in my mind. Sometimes my heart would bubble over with such sweet delight and was filled with such lightness, freedom, and consolation that I was totally transformed and enraptured. At other times I would be consumed with a burning love for Jesus Christ and for all of God's creation. Sometimes sweet tears of gratitude to the Lord, for His mercy to me a sinner, would pour out of me of their own accord.[14] And again, at times, my former foolish understanding was so illumined that suddenly I was able to ponder and comprehend so easily what previously I could not have even imagined. Sometimes the sweet warmth in my heart would overflow and spread through my entire being, so that I tenderly experienced the presence of God all about me. At other times I would experience the greatest inner joy from calling upon the name of Jesus Christ, and I truly began to understand the meaning of His words: "The Kingdom of God is within you."[15]

As I was experiencing these and other delightful consolations, I noticed that the effects of the prayer of the heart are manifested in three ways: in the spirit, in feelings, and through revelations. In the spirit there is the sweetness of God's love, inner peace, the rapture of the mind, purity of thought, and the delightful remembrance of God. In the feelings there is a pleasant warming of the heart, a sweet delight that fills all the limbs, the heart bubbling over with joy, an inner lightness and vitality, the delight of being alive, and an inner detachment from illness and offenses. Revelations bring enlightenment of the intellect, an understanding of Holy Scripture, a knowledge of the language of all creatures, a detachment from anxiety and care, a taste of the sweet delights of the interior spiritual life, and a conviction of the close presence of God and of His love for us.

❖ "Therefore from ancient times those who were zealous for salvation and experienced in the spiritual life—through God's inspiration and without relinquishing their ascetic struggle—discovered another way to warm the heart, which they have handed on for the use of others. This appears simpler and easier, but is in fact no less difficult to carry out. This shortcut to the achievement of our aim is the whole-hearted practice of inner prayer to our Lord and Savior. This is how it should be performed: stand with your mind and attention in your heart, being very sure that the Lord is near and listening, and call to Him with fervor: "Lord Jesus Christ, have mercy on me." Do this constantly in church and at home, traveling, working, at table, and in bed—in a word, from the time that you open your eyes till the time that you shut them. This will be exactly like holding an object in the sun, because this is to hold yourself before the face of the Lord, who is the Sun of the spiritual world. At the beginning, you must give up an allotted part of your time, night and morning, exclusively to this prayer. Then you will find that the prayer begins to bear fruit, as it lays hold of the heart and becomes deeply rooted in it."

—Bishop Theophan the Recluse (Russian, 1815–1891)

16 Irkutsk: See page 34.

17 Psalm 104:24.

I spent about five months in solitude engaged in this prayerful practice and enjoying the experiences I have described. I became so accustomed to the prayer of the heart that I practiced it continuously, until I finally felt that my mind and heart began to act and recite the prayer without any effort on my part. This continued not only when I was awake but even as I slept, and nothing could interrupt it. It did not stop for even a moment, no matter what I happened to be occupied with. My soul was filled with gratitude to the Lord, while my heart continued in unceasing joy.

The time came for cutting down the trees in the forest, and the workers began to arrive. And so, it was also time for me to leave my solitary abode. I thanked the forester, said a prayer, and knelt to kiss that plot of ground, which God had given to one as undeserving of His mercy as I am, to live on. I put my knapsack containing the books on my back and set out on my journey.

For a very long time I wandered through different places, until I arrived in Irkutsk.[16] The self-acting prayer of the heart was my consolation and joy throughout the journey and in all my encounters. It never ceased to delight me, though in varying degrees. Wherever I happened to be, whatever I was doing, it never got in the way and was never diminished in any way at all. If I was working, the prayer flowed from my heart on its own, and the work seemed to go by faster. If I was listening attentively to something or reading while the prayer continued unceasingly, I would simultaneously be aware of both, as if I'd been divided in two or as if there were two souls in my one body. O my God! What a mystery man is! "O Lord, how wondrous are thy works! In wisdom hast Thou made them all."[17]

My travels were also filled with many wonderful experiences and incidents. Were I to recount them all, twenty-four hours would not suffice!

18 Feast days: The pilgrim would thus have been interrupted fairly frequently in the course of a year, on the following twelve major feast days of the Orthodox Church:

- Nativity of the Virgin Mary: September 8
- Exaltation of the Cross: September 14
- Presentation of the Virgin in the Temple: November 21
- Nativity of Christ (Christmas): December 25
- Theophany, or the Baptism of Christ (Epiphany): January 6
- The Presentation of Christ in the Temple (Purification of Mary): February 2
- Annunciation: March 25
- Palm Sunday: one week before Pascha (Easter)
- Ascension: forty days after Pascha
- Pentecost: fifty days after Pascha
- Transfiguration of Christ: August 6
- Dormition (Falling Asleep) of the Virgin Mary (Assumption): August 15

In addition, large crowds would be expected on Easter, known as Pascha, and during the weeks preceding it, as well as on the feast day for which the church was named, or for the feast days of popular saints.

It is interesting to note that, up until the Russian Revolution, all of Russia used the Julian calendar, which by the mid-eighteenth century had been supplanted elsewhere in Europe as well as in America by the more accurate Gregorian calendar now universally in use for secular dates throughout the world. Though the Julian calendar (named for Julius Caesar and first adopted by the Romans in 46 B.C.E.) is virtually identical to the Gregorian (named for Pope Gregory XIII, who promulgated it in 1582), its ineffectual method for dealing with the few "extra" hours each solar year contains caused it to fall a few minutes short per year. By the nineteenth century it was twelve days behind the Gregorian calendar (today, at the beginning of the twenty-first century it is thirteen days behind). Thus, for example, when the pilgrim celebrated Christmas on December 25, it was January 6 in most of the rest of the world. The Orthodox Church in Russia continues to use the Julian calendar liturgically, though the greater part of Orthodox elsewhere follow the Gregorian.

❖

In the spring I came to a village where I found lodging for the night at a priest's house. The priest was a very kind man and lived all by himself, and I ended up spending three days with him. After he got to know me a bit during this time, he said, "Stay here with me. I need a conscientious man here, and I'll pay you. You see that we are building a new stone church, near the old wooden one. I have not been able to find a reliable man to serve as caretaker during the construction and to sit in the old church and be in charge of accepting donations for the new building. You could handle this, and it would suit your way of life, since it would allow you to sit alone in the chapel and pray. There is even a separate little booth for the caretaker to sit in. Please stay, at least until the new church is built." I tried to get out of doing this, but the priest was so insistent that finally I had to give in to his request.

Throughout that summer and into the fall I lived in the chapel. At first it was peaceful and very conducive to reciting my prayer, even though the chapel was much visited, especially on feast days.[18] Some people came to pray and some simply to pass the time, while others came to steal from the collection box. I regularly read the Bible and the *Philokalia*, and when visitors saw this, some of them would strike up a conversation with me. Others would simply ask me to read to them for a while.

I noticed that a young peasant girl came frequently to the chapel, on each visit spending a long time in prayer. I overheard some of her hushed words and found that some of the prayers she was using were very odd-sounding, while others seemed to be somewhat distorted versions of the ones with which I was familiar. "Who taught you all this?" I asked. She replied that her mother, who was a pious woman, had taught her. Her father was a schismatic who belonged to a sect that rejected the

19 The girl's father almost certainly belonged to one of the groups collectively known as Old Believers, or *raskolniki*.

The movement originated in 1666, when the Patriarch of Moscow, Nikon, introduced liturgical reforms into the Russian Orthodox Church intended to bring its practices in line with those of Orthodox Christians elsewhere. It is significant that the reforms had nothing to do with theology or doctrine, but were strictly liturgical, having to do with placement of the fingers when making the sign of the cross and with the number of prostrations performed with the prayer of St. Ephraim of Syria (see page 110). The Old Believers, under their saintly and charismatic leader Avvakum, refused to submit to the reformed practice, preferring their distinctly Russian practices, which were, in many cases, more ancient than the practices of their Greek-speaking contemporaries. They split into two main groups, the *popovsty* (those with priests) and the *bezpopovsty* (those without any priesthood, and with less in the way of formal organization in general), to which the girl's father likely belonged.

The Old Believers' communities endured into modern times, in spite of periods of persecution, and continue today. They represent the most significant schismatic movement in the history of the Orthodox Church.

20 The commonest of all the Orthodox prayers to the Virgin Mary, obviously related to the Catholic "Hail Mary," and repeated oftener than any prayer other than the "Our Father":

Rejoice, Virgin Theotokos [*see glossary*],
Mary full of grace, the Lord is with you.
Blessed are you among women,
And blessed is the fruit of your womb
For you have borne the Savior of our souls.

priesthood.[19] I sympathized with all this and then advised her to pray according to the proper tradition of the church: namely, the Lord's Prayer and "Rejoice, Virgin Theotokos."[20] Finally I said to her, "Why don't you make a habit of saying the Jesus prayer? It reaches out to God more directly than any other prayer, and through it you will attain salvation."

The girl took my advice to heart and very simply began doing what I had taught her. And do you know what happened? After a short time she informed me that she had become so accustomed to the Jesus prayer that she felt compelled to recite it continuously, if such a thing were possible, and that while she prayed she was filled with happiness, whereas when she stopped, she was filled with joy and a fervent desire to continue praying. I was overjoyed by this and advised her to keep praying in the name of Jesus Christ.

By the end of summer many of the visitors to the chapel were now coming to see me. They came not only to hear me read to them and for advice, but they also brought all their problems to me, even seeking help in locating misplaced or lost items. Obviously, some of them took me for some sort of fortune-teller.

As time went on, life became unbearably noisy for me and full of distracting temptations. Finally the summer was over, and I decided to leave the chapel and proceed on my journey. I went to the priest and said, "Father, you know what I seek. I need quiet surroundings in order to pray, and there are too many harmful distractions here. I have fulfilled my promise to you and have stayed through the summer. Let me go now, and give me your blessing for my solitary journey."

The priest did not want to let me go, and he tried to convince me to

21 Batushka: "Little Father." An affectionate term used in addressing a priest, but also sometimes used in addressing any respected older man.

22 Mount Athos, also called "the Holy Mountain," is a place referred to frequently in *The Way of a Pilgrim* and is often encountered in readings on Eastern Orthodox spirituality. It is a mountainous peninsula in northeastern Greece that is sometimes considered a kind of homeland of Orthodox monasticism. Since the tenth century, the peninsula has been inhabited solely by monks (and closed entirely to women), living in a variety of situations from large monasteries to tiny settlements. Today there are twenty monasteries on Athos, along with numerous smaller foundations called "sketes," and hermits living in caves and small huts. The largest number of the communities are Greek-speaking, but there are also communities of Russians, Romanians, Bulgarians, and Serbians. Athos has produced many of the most influential figures in Orthodox spirituality. An excellent illustrated book on Athos is *Anchored in God: Life, Art, and Thought on the Holy Mountain of Athos*, by Constantine Cavarnos (Belmont, Mass.: Institute for Byzantine and Modern Greek Studies, 1975).

23 Matthew 16:26.

stay. "What's stopping you from praying right here? There's nothing for you to do here except to sit in the chapel. Your daily bread is provided for you. Say your prayers there day and night, if you like, and live with God, brother! You are gifted, and your presence here is good for us. You don't gossip idly with visitors, and you are doing something profitable for God's church by faithfully taking in the collections. This is more pleasing to God than your prayers in solitude. What do you need solitude for? It's better to pray in community with others. God did not create man so that he could get to know only himself, but so that people would help each other and lead each other to salvation according to each one's abilities. Look at the examples of the saints and the Fathers! They were concerned and cared for the church day and night and traveled all over to preach. They did not go off in solitude and hide from people."

"God gives to each man his own gift, *Batushka*.[21] There have been many preachers, but there have also been many hermits. Each found his own unique calling and followed it, believing that through this God Himself was guiding him on the path to salvation. How then would you explain the fact that so many saints gave up their ecclesiastical offices, administrative positions, and priestly duties and fled into the solitude of the desert, to avoid the confusion and distractions of living among people? St. Isaac of Syria fled, leaving behind his diocese. The venerable Athanasius of Athos[22] fled from his large monastery. They did this precisely because those places were too distracting, too full of temptations for them, and because they genuinely believed the words of Jesus Christ: 'For what will it profit a man, if he gains the whole world and forfeits his life?'"[23]

"But they were saints!" said the priest.

"If the saints needed to protect themselves from the dangers of mingling with people," I replied, "then what must a poor sinner resort to?"

24 St. Anthony the Great (251–356) was the Egyptian hermit known as the "Father of Monasticism." His *Life*, written by St. Athanasius of Alexandria, made him famous throughout the Christian world and served as the inspiration for the monastic movement that became such a large phenomenon in the fourth century and after.

The text attributed to him, "On the Character of Men and on the Virtuous Life: One Hundred and Seventy Texts," opens the *Philokalia,* because, if Anthony is its author, it would be the oldest text in the chronologically arranged collection. But scholars now agree that the work was almost certainly not written by Anthony, and is probably not even of Christian origin to begin with. It is likely a compilation of excerpts from the works of various Stoic and Platonic writers from the first to the fourth centuries, C.E.

25 St. John of Karpathos: Few facts are known about the life of this author of the text entitled "For the Encouragement of the Monks in India Who Had Written to Him: One Hundred Texts"—a document intended to offer encouragement to those who were tempted to leave the monastic life.

Karpathos is a Greek island in the Sporades archipelago, between Crete and Rhodes. John of Karpathos is thought to have been a monk living in community, who went on to become bishop of his island, possibly in the seventh century. Despite the work's title, it is unlikely that he would have written Christian monks in India in the seventh century. Scholars speculate that the oddly titled document was addressed to monks in Ethiopia.

26 1 John 4:4.

27 1 Corinthians 10:13.

28 St. Gregory of Thessalonika: St. Gregory Palamas. See page 18.

In the end I finally parted from this kind priest, and he lovingly saw me on my way.

The weather was dry, and I had no desire to spend the night in another village. So that evening, when I saw two haystacks in the forest, I settled down under them for the night. As I slept I dreamed that I was walking along the road and reading chapters from the work of St. Anthony the Great[24] in the *Philokalia*. Suddenly my starets caught up with me and said, "You're reading the wrong passage. This is what you should read," and he pointed to the thirty-fifth chapter of St. John of Karpathos,[25] where I read the following: "Sometimes the teacher submits to humiliation and suffers temptations for the sake of those who will benefit spiritually from this." The starets also pointed out the forty-first chapter, by the same St. John, which said: "Those who pray most earnestly are the ones who are assailed by the most terrible and fierce temptations."

Then the starets said, "Be strong in spirit and do not despair! Remember what the apostle said: 'He who is in you is greater than he who is in the world.'[26] Now you have experienced for yourself that a man is tempted only as much as he can endure it; 'but with the temptation God will also provide the way of escape.'[27] Hoping in God's help is what strengthened holy men of prayer and led them on to zeal and fervor. Such men not only gave their lives over to unceasing prayer, but out of their love they also revealed and taught it to others, whenever the opportunity presented itself. St. Gregory of Thessalonika[28] says the following about this: 'It is not only we who should heed God's command to pray unceasingly in the name of Christ. We must also reveal and teach this prayer to others—to everyone, in fact: monastics, lay people, the wise, the simple, husbands, wives, and children. We must

29   Proverbs 18:19.

30   Relics: The saint's bodily remains. In the case of St. Innocent, his corpse would have been enclosed in an ornate shrine, before which the faithful would pray and make prostrations.

The veneration of relics is a practice that dates to the early Church and has remained strong throughout the Orthodox world. St. Cyril of Jerusalem (fourth century) writes in his *Catechetical Lectures* (18:16): "Though the soul is not present, a power resides in the bodies of the saints because of the righteous soul which has for so many years dwelt in it or used it as a minister."

awaken in them a desire to pray unceasingly.' The venerable Callistus Telicudis says something very similar: 'Neither mental prayer to the Lord [i.e., interior prayer] nor contemplative illumination nor any means of elevating one's soul should be hoarded in one's own mind. They must be recorded, written down, and made available to others for the sake of love and the common good of all.' The Scriptures themselves speak of this: 'Brother helped by brother is like a strong fortress.'[29] However, in this case one should flee vanity in every possible way and guard oneself, so that the seed of God's Word is not sown into the wind."

When I awakened, my heart was filled with great joy, my soul was strengthened, and I went on my way.

The prayer became an ever greater comfort to me, so that often my heart would bubble over with boundless love for Jesus Christ. Gentle streams of consolation would flow from this delight throughout the limbs and joints of my body. The remembrance of Jesus Christ was so engraved in my mind that when I meditated on biblical events it was as if I could see them right before my eyes. I was filled with a warm tenderness and shed tears of joy. An inexpressible joy filled my heart!

At times I would go for three whole days without encountering any human habitation, which, to my immense delight, made me feel as if I were the only person alive on earth—one poor sinner in the presence of the supremely merciful and loving God. This solitude consoled me and enabled me to experience the delights of the prayer with far greater sensitivity than I was able to experience when surrounded by people.

Finally I arrived in Irkutsk. After venerating the relics of St. Innocent,[30] I began consider what I should do next. I had no desire to stay in that big city much longer. As I was walking down the street lost in

31 Odessa, the major port of the Ukraine, and Constantinople, then the
capital of the Ottoman empire, faced each other across the Black Sea,
and a major shipping route runs between them. The Bosphorus, a narrow waterway dividing the European and Asian parts of Constantinople, provided the only water access to the Mediterranean Sea from
Russia. Pilgrims to Jerusalem traveled this route not only because it was
easier and safer than the land route, but because it enabled them to
visit Constantinople's many Christian shrines and churches on their way
to the Holy Land.

Though the city had been renamed Istanbul at its conquest by the
Ottoman Turks in 1453, Russians still nostalgically referred to it by the
name by which it had been known as the capital of the Christian Eastern Roman Empire.

thought I met one of the local merchants. He stopped me and asked, "Are you a pilgrim? Why don't you come over to my house?" I went, and soon we arrived at his elegant home. He asked me about myself, and I told him about my travels. When I had finished, he said, "It is to Jerusalem that you should make a pilgrimage. The shrines and relics there cannot compare to anything else in the world!"

"I would be happy to go there," I replied, "but there is no way to get there by land. I could get as far as the sea, but I don't have money to pay for a sea voyage."

"If you like," said the merchant, "I could make it possible for you to go. Just last year I sent an elderly friend there."

I fell at his feet, and he said, "Listen, I'll give you a letter of introduction to my son. He lives in Odessa and does business with Constantinople,[31] so his ships sail there. He will gladly arrange passage for you on one of his vessels. Then in Constantinople he will instruct his agents to book passage for you on another ship that sails to Jerusalem and to pay for it. It's not all that expensive."

When I heard this I was overcome with joy. I showered my benefactor with gratitude for his kindness. Then I thanked God for the fatherly love and care that He had bestowed on such a wretched sinner as I, who was no good to himself or to others, and who ate the bread of others in idleness.

I enjoyed the hospitality of the generous merchant for three days, and he provided me with the promised letter of introduction to his son. So there I was, on my way to Odessa, in hope of reaching the holy city of Jerusalem. Yet, I did not even know for sure if the Lord would grant me to venerate his life-giving tomb.

Third
Narrative

1 The identity of this person is unclear. It is not the pilgrim's late starets, but probably a spiritual director with whom he entered into a relationship some time after the starets's death. This second spiritual father is referred to throughout the third and fourth narratives.

2 Orlovsk province: An agricultural region just north of the Ukraine. A very long journey indeed by foot from Irkutsk.

3 Lying on top of the stove was not an unusual activity. A Russian stove, called a *kamin*, was a large brick structure central to the house, used for heating and cooking. Most included a kind of shelf above the oven or firebox, where one could lie to keep warm and where people, especially children, sometimes slept in winter.

Just before leaving Irkutsk I visited my spiritual father,[1] with whom I had spoken frequently, and said to him, "Well, now I am off to Jerusalem, and I've just come to say good-bye and to thank you for the love you have shown to me, an unworthy pilgrim."

"May God bless your journey," he replied. "But you know, you have not told me very much about yourself—who you are, where you are from. You've told me so much about your travels, I am curious to know where you lived and what you did before you became a pilgrim."

"Of course," I said. "I'll be glad to tell you about that too. My story is not a long one. I was born in a village in the Orlovsk province.[2] My parents died, leaving me and my older brother. He was ten years old at the time of their deaths, and I was almost three. Our grandfather took us in and raised us. He was a prosperous and honest old man who kept an inn on a main highway, and thanks to his kindness many a traveler stayed at the inn. My brother was very bold and often took off on his own, running around the village, while I spent more time at home with Grandfather. On feast days we attended church with him, and he often read from the Bible at home—from this very same Bible that I now carry with me, in fact. When my brother got older he began drinking heavily. I was seven years old at the time. Once, when we were lying down together on top of the stove,[3] he pushed me off and I hurt my left arm. I lost the use of this arm after that, and now it has withered up completely.

"Grandfather realized that I would not be able to work on the land, so he began to teach me to read and write. Since we had no grammar

❖ "Let us practice the prayer of Jesus disinterestedly, with simplicity
and purity of intention, with penitence as our objective, with faith in
God, with hope and trust in the wisdom, goodness, and omnipotence
of His holy will.... By attentive prayer let us seek to turn the gaze of our
mind to ourselves so that we may discover within ourselves our sinfulness. When we discover it, let us stand mentally before our Lord Jesus
Christ in the company of the lepers, the blind, the deaf, the lame, the
paralyzed, the possessed; and let us begin our mournful cry of prayer
before Him from the poverty of our spirit and from a heart crushed
with sorrow for our sinfulness. Let this cry be infinitely abundant. Let all
prolixity and all variety of words prove unfit to express it."

—Ignatius Brianchaninov, *On the Prayer of Jesus*, p. 113

4   "Have mercy on me, O God": The first line of Psalm 51, the Psalm
that begins the standard Orthodox morning and evening prayers and
which is the most frequently recited of all the Psalms among the Orthodox.

books, he somehow managed to use this very copy of the Bible instead. He started from the very beginning and had me writing words so I could learn the letters of the alphabet. I'm not sure how it happened, but by repeating everything he said, I eventually learned how to read. Later, when his vision grew poor, he often made me read to him from the Bible, correcting me as I went along.

"There was a regional clerk who often stayed at the inn, and he had such a beautiful handwriting. I enjoyed watching him write and tried to copy his writing. He began to teach me, giving me paper and ink and sharpening my pens. That was how I learned to write. Grandfather was very pleased by this and would say to me, 'Now that God has revealed reading and writing to you, it will make a man out of you. You must thank the Lord for this and pray more often.' So we would attend all the church services, but we also prayed a great deal at home. I would chant 'Have Mercy on me, O God,'[4] while Grandfather and Grandmother did their prostrations or simply knelt.

"Finally, when I turned seventeen, Grandmother died. Grandfather would say to me, 'We don't have a mistress of the house any longer—how are we going to manage without a woman? Your older brother has made a mess of his life, so I want you to get married.' I protested because of my disability, but Grandfather insisted. They found a serious and kind twenty-year-old girl for me, and we were married.

"One year later, Grandfather became ill and called for me from his deathbed. As he prepared to depart, he said, 'I am leaving you this house and everything I own. Live by your conscience, do not cheat anyone, and above all else pray to God, for everything comes from Him. Do not place your hope in anything or anyone, but only in God. Go to church, read the Bible, and remember me and the old lady in your prayers. I am giving you a thousand rubles. Be careful with the money and do not spend it foolishly, but do not be stingy with it either. Give to the church and to the poor.'

5 Fasting: There are many days of fasting for the Orthodox, and if the pilgrim and his wife observed them all, they would have spent a good deal of the year with an austere diet, including the following four annual fast periods:

- Great Lent: forty days before Pascha (Easter).
- The Apostles' Fast: a week after the movable feast of Pentecost, and ending with the feast of Saints Peter and Paul on June 29. Depending on the date of Pentecost in a particular year, the length of this fast can vary between one and six weeks.
- Dormition Fast: August 1 to 14, ending with the feast of the Falling Asleep of the Virgin Mary.
- The Nativity Fast: November 15 to December 24, ending with Christmas.

In addition, nearly every Wednesday and Friday of the year are fast days, and there are various one-day fasts, such as the eve of Theophany. During fast periods, pious Christians would abstain from meat, fish, poultry, eggs, dairy products, oil, and wine.

6 Akathist hymn: An akathist is an ancient form of hymnography consisting of fourteen hymns, each of which is followed by a series of statements of praise or thanksgiving. There are akathists written for Christ, the Virgin Mary, and for many different saints, but the most famous akathist of all, and the one to which the pilgrim refers, is the famous one to the Virgin, written by St. Romanos the Melodist. Its first section is thus:

An archangel was sent from Heaven to say to the Mother of God: Rejoice! And beholding You, O Lord, taking bodily form, he was amazed and with his bodiless voice he stood crying to Her such things as these:

Rejoice, You through whom joy will shine forth:
Rejoice, You through whom the curse will cease!
Rejoice, recall of fallen Adam:
Rejoice, redemption of the tears of Eve!
Rejoice, height inaccessible to human thoughts:
Rejoice, depth undiscernible even for the eyes of angels!

"So he died and I buried him. My brother grew jealous because I alone had inherited the inn and the rest of the estate. He became enraged with me and was so caught up in evil that he actually plotted to kill me. This is what he finally did one night, while my wife and I were sleeping. There were no guests at the inn, and he broke into the closet where I kept the money, stole it from the chest, and set fire to the closet. By the time we awakened, the fire had spread throughout the inn. We barely managed to jump out the window to safety, wearing nothing but our nightclothes.

"Since we kept the Bible under our pillows, we were able to take it with us. As we stood and watched our house burning we said to each other, 'Thank God that we were at least able to rescue the Bible! At least we have something to console us in our distress.' Thus our entire estate burned down, and my brother disappeared without a trace. Much later we found out that he had begun to drink heavily and had been heard to boast about how he stole the money and set fire to the inn.

"We were left completely destitute, without any clothing or even a pair of shoes to wear. Somehow we managed to borrow some money to build a small cabin, and we started living in it as landless peasants. My wife did beautiful handiwork—weaving, spinning, and sewing. She took in work, laboring day and night to support us. With my withered arm I could not even make shoes, so I would sit while she did her work and read to her from the Bible. As she listened, from time to time she would be moved to tears. 'Why are you crying?' I'd ask. 'Thank God that at least we are alive.' And she would reply, 'The Bible contains such beautiful words that it touches me deeply.'

"Remembering Grandfather's admonitions, we fasted frequently,[5] chanted the *akathist* hymn[6] to the Theotokos every morning, and did one thousand prostrations before going to bed at night, so as not to fall into temptation. Thus we lived peacefully for two years. It is interesting that although we had never heard of the prayer of the heart, did

Rejoice, for you are the throne of the King:
Rejoice, for Thou bear Him Who bears all!
Rejoice, star that causes the Sun to appear:
Rejoice, womb of the Divine Incarnation!
Rejoice, You through whom creation is renewed:
Rejoice, You through whom we worship the Creator!
Rejoice, Bride Unwedded!

7 "Last Communion": The sacrament of Holy Communion was received by most Christians of nineteenth-century Russia infrequently, usually no more than a time or two per year, and was preceded by a period of fasting and preparation. Because the sacrament was believed to bring forgiveness of sins, it was thought beneficial to receive it on one's deathbed.

8 "Permanent disability passport": In the pilgrim's time a passport was required for Russians traveling even within Russia.

9 Kiev: The object of this pilgrimage would have been the Pecherskaya Lavra, or Monastery of the Caves, a monastery founded in the twelfth century whose caves contain many relics of the saintly monks who lived there.

not understand it, and simply prayed with our lips, doing mindless prostrations like fools turning somersaults, we still had the desire to pray. Not only was it easy for us to recite long prayers without really understanding them, but we did so with great delight. It seems that teacher was right when he told me that one could pray secretly within himself, without being consciously aware of the prayer or of how it acts on its own in the soul and awakens the desire to pray, according to each person's knowledge and ability.

"After we had lived this way for two years, my wife suddenly became ill with a very high fever. She received her last Communion[7] and died on the ninth day of her sickness. I was left completely alone, without any means of supporting myself. So I started wandering about and begging, which made me quite ashamed. In addition, I was so overcome by grief over losing my wife that I didn't know what to do with myself. When I walked into my cabin and saw her clothing or a kerchief she had worn, I would begin to cry. Finally it became impossible for me to bear the grief of living at home. So I sold my hut for twenty rubles and gave all my wife's remaining clothing to the poor. Because of my arm, I was given a permanent disability passport,[8] and I took my Bible and set off without any particular destination in mind.

"'Where will I go now?' I thought. 'I'll go to Kiev first, to venerate the relics of God's worthy saints and ask for their help and intercession.'[9] This decision instantly made me feel much better, and my journey to Kiev was a happy one. This was thirteen years ago, and ever since then I have been wandering. I have visited many churches and monasteries, but these days I keep mainly to the steppes and fields. I am not sure if it is the Lord's will for me to reach the holy city. If it is God's will, perhaps it will also be time for my sinful bones to be buried there."

"How old are you now?" he asked.

"I'm thirty-three," I replied.

"The age of Jesus Christ at His death!"

A woodcut representation of the monastery of the Kiev Caves, with its founders, Saints Anthony and Theodosius

Fourth
Narrative

But for me it is good to be near God;
I have made the Lord God my refuge.

—PSALM 73:28

I came to my spiritual father and said, "How true is the Russian proverb: 'Man proposes, but God disposes.' I had planned to set out today and start on my pilgrimage to Jerusalem. But something altogether unexpected occurred that has kept me here for three more days. I could not resist coming here to tell you about it, for I need your advice on what to do.

"After I had said good-bye to everyone, with God's help I set out on my journey. Just as I was about to pass through the gates of the city, I saw a familiar man standing at the doorway of the last house. He was once a pilgrim, just as I am now, and I had not seen him for three years. We greeted each other, and he asked me where I was headed.

"I replied, 'I'd like to get to the holy city of Jerusalem, God willing.'

"'Thank God!' he exclaimed. 'I have an excellent traveling companion for you!'

"'God be with you and with him,' I said, 'but you must remember that I never travel with anyone, since I'm used to walking alone.'

"'Hear me out—I know that this traveling companion will be just right for you. You will both suit each other quite nicely. You see, the father of the master of the house where I work has also made a vow to see Jerusalem. You will get used to each other, I assure you. He's a local man, of the lower middle class, elderly and really quite deaf. So it does not matter how much you shout at him, he won't hear anything. If you need to speak with him, you must write down what you want to say on paper, and he'll answer you. So he won't bother you on the journey,

❖ "The chief and beginning of all virtues is prayer, of which the Apostle has said: 'Pray without ceasing.' That is, always call upon the name of God, whether when conversing, when sitting down, when walking, when working, when eating, or whenever doing anything else. At all times and in every place it is fitting to call upon the name of God; for thus we 'Beat the enemies,' says St. John of the Ladder, 'with the name of Jesus,' and a stronger weapon you will not find either in heaven or earth.

"Prayer is the banishing of sorrow and depression, the blossoming of meekness and angerlessness, the manifestation of joy and thanksgiving, and the obtaining and multiplying of countless good things.

"I hope that you will prosper in virtues, and this will be the case above all if you live in heedfulness and do not neglect the prayer of Jesus. For it is the chief and beginning of all virtues. There is nothing that so much guards against the entry of the evil demon than prayer (the mental prayer of Jesus) and fervent entreaty."

—Elder Hilarion of Valaam Monastery (died 1841),
from "A Short Spiritual Ladder" (*Little Russian Philokalia*,
vol. 2. Platina, Calif.: St. Herman Brotherhood, 1983, p. 77)

1 Philippians 2:13.

because he won't be talking to you. He hardly speaks even in his own home, but you would be indispensable to him on the journey. His son is providing him with a horse and wagon to get to Odessa, where he will sell both. The old man would prefer to go on foot, but he needs the horse for his luggage and some packages he is taking to the Lord's tomb, and you could load your knapsack on his wagon.

"'Think about it! How can you let an old, deaf man go off on his own, in a horse-drawn wagon, on such a long journey? We have been looking for some time for a traveling companion for him, but they're all asking too much money. And it would dangerous to send him off with a total stranger, especially since he's carrying money and parcels with him. Please say yes, brother; I assure you all will be well. Do this to the glory of God and for love of your fellow man. I will recommend you to the old man's family, and they will be overjoyed to hear about you. They are kind people and care a great deal for me. I've been working for them for two years.'

"We had been standing and talking at the entrance to the house. He took me inside and introduced me to the master. I realized that this was an honest and good family, so I agreed. We decided to leave, God willing, on the third day after Christmas, immediately after the Divine Liturgy.

"You see what kinds of coincidences happen in one's life! Yet, God and His divine Providence always guide all our plans and deeds, just as it is written: 'For God is at work in you, both to will and to work for his good pleasure.'"[1]

My spiritual father listened to my story and said, "I rejoice with all my heart, dearest brother, that the Lord has willed for me to see you again, so soon and so unexpectedly. Since you have some free time on your hands, I lovingly ask you to remain with me a little while longer and tell me more about the edifying experiences you have had during

2   Philippians 3:13.

❖   "This stillness or inward silence is known in Greek as *hesychia*, and he who seeks the prayer of stillness is termed a *hesychast*. Hesychia signifies concentration combined with inward tranquillity. It is not merely to be understood in a negative sense as the absence of speech and outward activity, but it denotes in a positive way the openness of the human heart towards God's love. Needless to say, for most people if not all, hesychia is not a permanent state. The hesychast, as well as entering into the prayer of stillness, uses other forms of prayer as well, sharing in corporate liturgical worship, reading Scripture, receiving the sacraments. Apophatic prayer coexists with cataphatic, and each strengthens the other. The way of negation and the way of affirmation are not alternatives; they are complementary."

—Kallistos Ware, *The Orthodox Way,* pp. 163–164

your pilgrimages. I have listened with such pleasure and delight to all your other stories."

"I will be more than happy to do so," I replied, and I began to talk.

So many things, good and bad, have happened to me, that it would not be possible for me to tell you about them all. I'm sure I've even forgotten some, for my attention was always more focused on what was guiding and prodding my lazy soul to pray. So I did not spend much time thinking about anything else—or, rather, I tried to forget the past, as the Apostle Paul teaches us, saying: "forgetting what lies behind and straining forward to what lies ahead."[2] Even my late starets of blessed memory would tell me that obstacles to the prayer of the heart come from two sources: from the left and from the right. This means that if the enemy fails to prevent us from praying through vain thoughts and sinful imaginations, then he stirs within us memories of all kinds of edifying things, or he entices us with pleasant thoughts—anything at all to tempt us away from prayer, which is something he cannot bear.

This is what is called "right-hand theft," and it causes the soul to scorn converse with God and to turn to the pleasure of conversing with its own self or with other creatures. Therefore, he taught me that during prayer I must reject even the most pleasant spiritual thoughts. Moreover, he taught me that if I should happen to notice during the course of a day that I am spending more time on edifying speculation or conversation than on the essential hidden prayer of the heart, I should consider even this as being immoderate, or as a form of self-seeking spiritual gluttony. This applies especially to beginners, for whom it is vital that the time they spend on prayer must significantly exceed even the time they spend on any other pious activities.

3 Tobolsk: An Asian Russian city in the plains just east of the Ural Mountains.

4 Pilgrims could, in general, expect to be treated well, since there were enough people who considered the care of pilgrims a blessing. The level of hospitality shown by the well-to-do family he encounters later in this narrative would have been extraordinary.

But one cannot forget all the rest, either. It can happen that an experience becomes so ingrained in one's mind that even if one does not think about it often, it remains etched in memory. A case in point would be the pious family with whom God granted me to once spend a few days.

While I was traveling I happened to pass through a city of the province of Tobolsk.[3] I was down to the last of my dried bread, so I stopped at a house to ask for some. The master of the house said to me, "Thank God that you have come at the right moment! My wife has just taken some fresh bread out of the oven. Here is a warm loaf for you; pray to God for us."[4] I thanked him and started to put the bread in my knapsack when the mistress of the house saw me and said, "Look at your knapsack—it's all worn out! Let me give you another one." And she gave me a good, sturdy one in its place. I thanked them with all my heart and went on my way. On the way out of the city, I stopped in a little shop and asked for some salt. The shopkeeper gave me a small bagful, and I rejoiced in spirit, thanking God for bringing me in my unworthiness to such kind people. Now I would not have to worry about food for a whole week. I could sleep peacefully and be satisfied. Bless the Lord, O my soul!

I had walked about three and a half miles beyond the city when I came across a poor village along that road. There stood a wooden church, simple but nicely decorated with frescoes on the outside. As I walked past it I felt a desire to go inside and worship, so I went on the porch and prayed for a while. Two children, aged five or six, were playing on the grass alongside the church. I thought they were the priest's children, even though they were quite nicely dressed. But I said my prayers and went on my way. I had walked only ten steps away from the church when I heard shouting behind me: "Dear beggar! Dear beggar, wait!" The children, a boy and a girl, had seen me and were running toward me and shouting. I stopped, and they ran up to me and each

❖ "Sitting in your cell, remain patiently in prayer, according to the precept of the Apostle Paul (Romans 12:12, Colossians 4:2). Collect your mind into your heart and send out thence your mental cry to our Lord Jesus, calling for His help and saying: 'Lord Jesus Christ, have mercy upon me.' Do not give in to faintheartedness and laziness, but labor in your heart and drive your body, seeking the Lord in your heart. Compel yourself by every means to do this work, for 'The kingdom of heaven suffereth violence, and the violent take it by force' (Matthew 11:12), as the Lord said showing that this attainment demands severe labor and spiritual struggle."

—from the *Philokalia*: St. Gregory of Sinai, "Instructions to Hesychasts"

grabbed one of my hands. "Come with us to Mama—she loves beggars," they said.

"I am not a beggar," I replied. "I'm just a man passing through."

"Then why do you have a knapsack?" they asked.

"I keep bread for my travels in there. But tell me, where is your mama?" I asked.

"She's over there, behind the church, just behind that little grove of trees."

They then led me into a beautiful garden, in the middle of which stood a large manor house. We went inside, and how immaculate everything was within! The mistress of the house ran out to meet us.

"Welcome! Welcome! From where has God sent you to us? Sit down, kind sir, sit down!" She removed the knapsack from my back, put it on the table, and sat me down in one of the softest chairs. "Wouldn't you like something to eat, or some tea? Is there anything at all that you need?"

"Thank you most humbly," I replied. "I have a sack full of food. Although I do sometimes drink tea, we peasants are not all that used to it. Your eagerness to help me and your loving welcome are more precious to me than any refreshments. I will pray to God that He bless you for the biblical spirit of your love of pilgrims." When I had said this I experienced an intense desire to enter into my inner self again. The prayer was kindled in my heart and I needed peace and silence, so I could give rein to this self-kindling flame of prayer and keep others from seeing the external signs that accompany it, such as tears, sighs, and the unusual facial gestures and movements of my lips. So I got up and said, "Please excuse me, dear mother, it's time for me to leave. May the Lord Jesus Christ be with you and with your kind children."

"Oh, no! God forbid that you go—I won't permit it! My husband will be coming home from the city this evening—he is a judge there—

5 | Icon room: Icons, or holy images of Jesus, Mary, and the saints, were much venerated, but in the years before mass-produced prints, they were very expensive items, and very few could afford to have a room filled with them. The fact that the house contained an icon room or chapel is a sign of the family's wealth.

The theology of the image is very highly developed in the Eastern Church, as a result of a controversy over the use of icons that had the Eastern Roman Empire in upheaval between the years 725 and 843. A good introduction to the theology of the icon is *The Art of the Icon: A Theology of Beauty* by Paul Evdokimov (Torrance, Calif.: Oakwood Publications, 1989).

6 | Schema nun: The female equivalent of a schema monk (see page 8).

7 | The book would be *The Ladder of Divine Ascent* by St. John Climacus (circa 525–606), abbot of the Monastery of St. Catherine at Mount Sinai. This treatise, in which he describes thirty steps that take a person to God, was very popular spiritual reading in Russia. It is available in English translation as *John Climacus: The Ladder of Divine Ascent*, translated by Colm Luibheid (Mahwah, N.J.: Paulist Press, 1988).

8 | Matushka: "Little Mother." A respectful term of endearment most often used in addressing a priest's wife, but also sometimes used toward any older or respected woman, as here.

he'll be so happy to meet you! He regards every pilgrim as a messenger of God. If you leave now he will be very upset not to have seen you. Besides, tomorrow is Sunday, and you can pray at the Liturgy with us, and then we'll eat together as God provides. We always have guests on the feast days—as many as thirty of Christ's needy ones. But you have not even told me anything about yourself—where you come from and where you are going! Stay and talk with me, I love to hear about spiritual matters from devout people. Children, children! Take the pilgrim's knapsack and put it in the icon room[5]—that's where he will spend the night."

I was surprised by what she was saying and thought to myself: is this a human being, or is she some kind of apparition? So I stayed to meet the master of the house. I briefly told her about my journey and that I was headed for Irkutsk.

"Well, then," said the mistress, "you will have to pass through Tobolsk. My mother is a schema nun[6] now and lives in a monastery there. We will give you a letter of introduction, and she will receive you. Many people go to her for spiritual counsel. By the way, you can also take to her a book by St. John Climacus,[7] which she asked us to order from Moscow. How well all this fits together!"

Finally it was time for dinner, and we all sat down at the table, where four more women joined us. After the first course, one of them got up from the table and bowed to the icon, then to us. She served the second course and sat down again. Then another of the women repeated this and served the third course. Observing all this, I asked the mistress of the house, "If I may ask, *Matushka*,[8] are these ladies related to you?"

"Yes," she said, "they are sisters to me: this one is the cook, this one is the coachman's wife, that one is the housekeeper, and the last is my maid. They are all married—I don't have any unmarried girls working in my house."

❖ "Intelligent silence is the mother of prayer, a recall from captivity, preservation of fire, an overseer of thoughts, a watch against enemies, a prison of mourning, a friend of tears, effective remembrance of death, a depicter of punishment, a deliverer unto judgment, a minister of sorrow, an enemy of freedom of speech, a companion of stillness, an opponent of the desire to teach, increase of knowledge, a creator of divine vision, unseen progress, secret ascent."

—from *The Ladder of Divine Ascent* by St. John Climacus, Step 11: "On talkativeness and silence" (Brookline, Mass.: Holy Transfiguration Monastery, 1978), p. 92

9 The lady's wealth and influence are indicated by the fact that she had special accommodations built for herself in the monastery, rather than occupying an ordinary nun's cell.

Having observed and listened to everything, I was even more astonished. I thanked God for bringing me to such devout people, and I experienced the intense activity of the prayer in my heart. Since I was eager
to be alone so as not to hinder the prayer, I got up from the table and
said to the mistress, "No doubt you will need to rest after dinner. I am
used to taking a walk, so I will stroll around the garden."

"No," she replied, "I do not need to rest. I will walk with you in the
garden, and you will tell me something soul-profiting. If you go alone,
the children will pester you. As soon as they see you, they won't leave
you for a moment, because they truly love the needy brethren of Christ
and pilgrims."

There was nothing I could do but go with her. In order to avoid having to talk myself, when we entered the garden, I bowed to the ground
before the mistress and said, "Matushka, in the name of God, please
tell me how long you have been living such a devout life and how you
achieved such piety."

"Perhaps I should tell you the whole story of my life. You see, my
mother is the great-granddaughter of St. Joasaph, whose relics lie in Bel-
gorod and are exposed for veneration. We used to own a large town
house and rented one wing of it to a nobleman, who was not too well off
financially. When he died, his widow was pregnant, and then she died
after giving birth. My mother had compassion on the poor orphaned
child and took him in to raise him. I was born one year later. We grew
up together, studied under the same tutors, and became as close as
brother and sister. Some time later my father died, and my mother
moved from the city to live here in the country on her estate. When
we grew up, my mother gave me in marriage to this orphaned young
man who had grown up in our house. She left us her entire estate and
entered a monastery, where she had a cell built for herself.[9] In giving
us her blessing, she admonished us to live as Christians, to pray

10 Kiss of peace: Three kisses—symbolic of the Holy Trinity—the first on the right cheek, the second on the left, and the third again on the right. A common pious greeting, seen especially at Pascha, or Easter.

11 Menaion: In this case, a book containing lives of the saints for the entire year, arranged according to their day of commemoration. The complete set of twelve volumes of the Orthodox service books is also called the Menaion.

12 St. John Chrysostom (circa 347–407): Reform-minded patriarch of Constantinople from 398 to 403, renowned as a preacher (hence his nickname, *Chrysostom*—"golden mouth" in Greek), and author of the Divine Liturgy celebrated by Orthodox Christians to this day. The book would likely have been a collection of his many recorded sermons.

earnestly to God, and above all else to strive to fulfill the most important of God's commandments: to love our neighbors and to feed and help those in need, with simplicity and humility to raise our children in the fear of God, and to treat our servants as though they were our brothers and sisters. So we have lived here by ourselves these last ten years, trying our best to follow our mother's instructions. We have a guesthouse for the poor, where there are more than ten crippled and needy people living at the moment. Perhaps tomorrow we will visit them."

When she had finished her story I asked, "Where is that book by St. John Climacus that you wanted delivered to your mother?"

"Let's go inside and I will find it for you."

No sooner had we sat down to read than the master of the house arrived. Upon seeing me he embraced me warmly, and we exchanged the kiss of peace.[10] Then he took me into his own room and said, "Come, dear brother, to my study and bless my cell. I think that you have had enough of her"—he pointed to his wife. "As soon as she sees a pilgrim or someone who is ill, she is more than glad to spend all day and night with them. Her entire family has been this way for generations." We went into his study. There were so many books and magnificent icons there, as well as a large cross with a life-sized figure of Christ on it and a Bible beside it. I prayed and then said to him: "Sir, what you have here is truly paradise. Here is the Lord Jesus Christ Himself, His most pure Mother, and His holy saints; and these"—I pointed to the books—"are their divinely inspired, living words and teachings, which can never be silenced. I would expect that you enjoy frequent spiritual converse with them."

"Yes, it's true," said the master. "I do love to read."

"What sort of books do you have here?" I asked.

"I have many spiritual books," he replied. "Here is the *Menaion*[11] for the entire year, and the works of St. John Chrysostom[12] and St.

13 St. Basil the Great (circa 330–379): Highly educated monk and bishop from Cappadocia in Anatolia (present-day central Turkey), who wrote a very influential rule for monks. He is, with Saints Gregory the Theologian and Gregory Nazianzus, one of the three "Cappadocian Fathers." The book would likely have been his *Letters*, or possibly his treatise "On the Holy Spirit."

Basil the Great.[13] There are many theological and philosophical works, as well as collections of many sermons of the most recent and celebrated preachers. My library is worth five thousand rubles."

"By any chance, would you have a book about prayer?" I asked.

"I love to read about prayer. Here is the most recent work on that subject, written by a priest in St. Petersburg." He reached for a volume on the Lord's Prayer, which we began to read aloud with pleasure.

Some time later, the mistress of the house brought us tea, while the children brought in a silver basket filled with pastries such as I had never seen before. The husband took the book from me, gave it to his wife, and said, "Since she reads so beautifully, we will have her read to us while we have some refreshment." She started reading, and we listened. As I listened to her I was able simultaneously to attend to the prayer in my heart. The more she read, the stronger the prayer became and the more it filled me with delight. Suddenly, it seemed to me as if someone passed before my eyes in a flash, through the air—as if it were my late starets. I shuddered, but not wanting them to notice this, I quickly said, "Forgive me, I must have dozed off." At that moment I felt as if the spirit of my starets had penetrated my own spirit, as if he had illumined it. I experienced a certain enlightenment in my understanding, and a multitude of thoughts about prayer came to me. I had just made the sign of the cross over myself in an attempt to banish these thoughts when the mistress finished reading the book. Her husband asked me if I had enjoyed it, and we began to discuss it.

"I liked it very much," I replied. "The Lord's Prayer—the Our Father—is more exalted and more precious than all the recorded prayers we Christians have, for it was given to us by the Lord Jesus Christ Himself. The commentary on it was very good, except that it focuses primarily on Christian works. In my reading of the holy Fathers, I have read also the contemplative, mystical commentaries on this prayer."

14 Maximus the Confessor (580–662): An extremely important Orthodox theologian whose particular concern was the place of humankind in theology. He was known as an eloquent refuter of the numerous heretical movements of his time. The host is certainly referring to Maximus' treatise "On the Lord's Prayer," which is found in the *Philokalia*.

15 St. Peter of Damascus: Very little is known of this figure whose writings occupy more space in the *Philokalia* than any other. Based on the time periods of the authors he cites, he is not likely to have lived before the eleventh century, but biographical details do not exist.

"In which of the Fathers did you read this?" he asked.

"Well, for example, in St. Maximus the Confessor[14] and, in the *Philokalia*, in the section by St. Peter Damascene."[15]

"Do you remember anything you read? Please, tell us about it!"

"Certainly! Let's take the first words of the prayer: *Our Father, Who art in heaven.* In the book we read today the interpretation of these words is to be understood as a call to love one's neighbor, since we are all children of the one Father. This is true, but the Fathers explain it further, on a deeper spiritual level. They say that the words are a call to raise the mind to heaven, to the heavenly Father, and to remember our obligation to place ourselves and live our lives in the presence of God at each and every moment. The words *hallowed be Thy Name* are explained in your book as being a sign of reverence, so that the Name of God would never be uttered disrespectfully or in vain. In a word, the holy Name of God must be spoken reverently and not taken in vain. The mystical commentators see these words as a direct request for the gift of interior prayer of the heart—a request that the most holy Name of God be engraved upon the heart and hallowed by the self-acting prayer, so that it might sanctify all our feelings and spiritual powers.

"The words *Thy Kingdom come* are explained by mystical commentators like this: may inner peace, tranquility, and spiritual joy come into our hearts. Your book explains the words *give us this day our daily bread* as a request for the material needs of our bodies—not in excess, but enough to fill our own needs and enough for us to be able to minister to the needy.

"However, St. Maximus the Confessor interprets 'daily bread' to mean the feeding of the soul with heavenly bread—the Word of God—and the union of the soul with God, through constant remembrance of Him and through the unceasing interior prayer of the heart."

"Ah! That is a great deed, but it is almost impossible for those who

❖ "Unceasing calling upon the name of God cures one not only of passions, but also of actions; and as a medicine affects a sick man without his comprehension, similarly the invocation of the name of God destroys passions in a manner beyond our comprehension."

—St. Barsanuphius the Great

❖ "The more rain falls on the earth, the softer it makes it; similarly, Christ's holy name gladdens the earth of our heart the more we call upon it."

—St. Hesychios the Priest

16 The work is entitled "A Treasury of Divine Knowledge."

live in the world to attain to interior prayer!" he exclaimed. "We're lucky when, with the Lord's help, we can simply say our prayers without laziness!"

"Don't look at it that way, sir. If it were so impossible and overwhelmingly difficult, the Lord would never have instructed us do it. His strength is made perfect also in weakness. From their own experience the Fathers offer us ways and methods that make it easier for us to attain to the prayer of the heart. Of course, they do teach special, more advanced methods for hermits, but they also prescribe convenient methods that serve as reliable guides for laypeople in attaining the prayer of the heart."

"I have never come across anything as detailed as this in my reading," said the master.

"Please, if you like, I will read to you from the *Philokalia*." I went to get my *Philokalia*, found the article by St. Peter of Damascus in section 3,[16] and read the following passage: "'More important than attending to breathing, one must learn to call upon the name of God at all times, in all places, and during all manner of activity. The apostle says: pray without ceasing; that is, he teaches constant remembrance of God at all times, in all places, and under any circumstances. If you are busy doing something, you must remember the Creator of all things; if you see light, remember Him who gave it to you. If you look at the sky, the earth, the waters, and all that is in them, marvel and glorify the Creator of all. If you are putting your clothes on, remember Him Whose gift they are, and thank Him Who provides everything in your life. In short, let every action be an occasion for you always to remember and praise God. And before you know it, you are praying unceasingly, and your soul will always rejoice in this.' Do you see now how this method for achieving unceasing prayer is convenient, easy, and accessible to any person who has at least some measure of human feelings?"

17   The "Akathist to the Most Sweet Jesus" follows the fourteen-section akathist model, beginning with this first section:

Creator of Angels and Lord of Hosts, as of old You opened the ear and tongue of him that was deaf and dumb, so now open my perplexed mind and tongue to praise Your most holy Name, that I may cry to You:

Jesus, most wonderful, Astonishment of Angels!
Jesus, most powerful, Deliverance of Forefathers!
Jesus, most sweet, Exultation of Patriarchs!
Jesus, most glorious, Dominion of kings!
Jesus, most desired, Fulfillment of Prophets!
Jesus, most praised, Steadfastness of Martyrs!
Jesus, most gladsome, Comfort of Monastics!
Jesus, most compassionate, Sweetness of Presbyters!
Jesus, most merciful, Abstinence of Fasters!
Jesus, most tender, Joy of the Righteous!
Jesus, most pure, Sobriety of Virgins!
Jesus, pre-eternal, Salvation of Sinners!
Jesus, Son of God, have mercy on me!

18   John 13:3–20.

They were very impressed by all this. The master embraced me with delight and thanked me. Then he looked through my *Philokalia* and said, "I will order this from Petersburg as soon as I can. But for now, let me copy this passage so I won't forget it. Please read it to me again." He wrote it down quickly and neatly. Then he exclaimed, "My God! Why, I even have an icon of the holy Damascene!" He picked up a picture frame, inserted the handwritten sheet behind the glass, and hung it beneath the icon. "There," he said, "the living word of God's saint, hanging right under his image. It will serve to remind me always to put his redemptive advice into practice."

After this we sat down to dinner, and the same people as before sat with us, men and women. What reverent silence and peace there was at that table! After the meal we all, adults and children, spent a long time in prayer. I was asked to chant the "Akathist to the Most Sweet Jesus."[17]

After prayers the servants went to bed, while the three of us remained in the room. The mistress brought me a white shirt and stockings. I made a prostration before her and said, "Dear mother, I will not take the stockings, for I have never worn such things in all my life. Peasants like me are used to wrapping our feet in strips of coarse linen." She hurried out of the room and brought back an old robe of hers, made of thin yellow fabric, and ripped it in half to make two strips. "Look," said the master, "the poor man's footwear is falling apart." He brought a pair of his own overshoes that were new and in a large size, the kind that are worn over boots. "Go in that empty room and change your clothes," he said. I did so, and when I returned they made me sit down and began to change my shoes. The husband wrapped the strips of cloth around my feet, while his wife pulled overshoes on top of them. At first I protested, but they insisted, saying, "Sit and be quiet—Christ washed the feet of His apostles."[18] I could do nothing but burst into tears. They wept with me. Afterward, the mistress retired for the night

19   The altar in Orthodox churches corresponds to what might be called the sanctuary in Western churches: the area in which the Eucharist is celebrated and toward which all the congregants face. This area is separated from the nave (the larger part of the church, where the congregants stand) by a screen covered with icons, called the iconostasis. The iconstasis contains three doors: the central or "royal doors"— double doors, through which only clergy pass—and two smaller single doors, one on either side. The woman and her daughters may have been standing by one of these smaller "deacon doors" to get a glimpse of what went on inside the altar. Women were not ordinarily admitted behind the iconostasis—nor were men who were not clergy or who were not serving as acolytes. Thus, it is unusual that the pilgrim and his host stood there during the service.

The elevation of Gifts to which the pilgrim refers is the moment during the prayers when the priest standing at the altar raises the bread and wine in offering to God.

20   The woman's name was Maria, of which "Masha" is a diminutive.

with the children, while the master and I went to the summerhouse in the garden.

For a long time we did not feel sleepy, so we lay awake and talked.

After our conversation the master and I slept for an hour or so, until we heard the bell for matins. We got up and went to church. Just as we walked inside we saw the mistress, who had been there for some time already with the children. We stood through matins and then the Divine Liturgy, which followed soon after. The master and I stood with the little boy in the altar, while his wife and daughter stood near the altar door so they could observe the elevation of the Gifts.[19] My, how they prayed as they knelt, with tears of joy streaming down their faces! They all looked so radiant that just watching them brought forth the fullness of my own tears.

After the Liturgy the nobles, the priest, the servants, and all the beggars went to the dining room of my hosts' house to eat. There were some forty beggars, and everyone—the crippled, the infirm, children—were all seated at one table. How tranquil it was! Summoning my boldness, I quietly said to the master, "In monasteries they read from the lives of the saints during meals. Since you have the complete Menaion, you could do the same." He turned to his wife and said, "Actually, Masha,[20] why don't we start doing that regularly? It would be most edifying. I will read first, at this meal, then you can read at the next, and then the father can read. After that, whoever else knows how to read can take turns."

The priest, who was still eating, said, "I love to listen, but as for reading, well, with all due respect, I do not have the time for it. The minute I get home I have so much to do, so many duties and concerns to attend to, I hardly know where to begin. First one thing needs to be

21 By canon, or Church, law, priests are not permitted to remarry after their wives die—they can, in fact, marry only once, and that must occur before their ordination. So this priest would have been celibate by requirement.

22 Nikitas Stethatos (circa 1000–circa 1092): monk and priest of Constantinople, biographer of St. Symeon the New Theologian (see page 16) and also his disciple. The selection quoted is from "On the Practice of the Virtues: One Hundred Texts."

23 Presanctified Gifts: A portion of the bread and wine of Communion is reserved and kept on the altar table, to be brought to the sick. A pious Orthodox Christian would want to receive the Presanctified Gifts just before dying—which is why the priest goes to get them "just to be on the safe side."

done, then another; then there are all the children, and the cows need to be let out. My days are so completely filled that I'm not up to reading or study. I've long since forgotten even what I learned at seminary." When I heard this I shuddered, but the mistress, who was sitting next to me, grasped my hand and said, "Father speaks this way from humility. He always humbles himself, but he is the most righteous and kindest of men. He has been a widower for twenty years now and has been raising a whole family of grandchildren, as well as serving frequent services in church."[21] Her words reminded me of the following saying of Nikitas Stethatos[22] in the *Philokalia*: "The nature of things is measured by the interior disposition of the soul; that is, the kind of person one is will determine what he thinks of others." He goes on to say: "He who has attained a genuine prayer and love no longer puts things into categories. He does not separate the righteous from the sinners, but loves all equally and does not judge them, just as God gives the sun to shine and the rain to fall both on the just and the unjust."

This was followed again by silence. A blind beggar from the guest-house sat across from me. The master fed him, cutting up his fish for him and handing him a spoon filled with broth. I noticed that the beggar's mouth was constantly open and his tongue kept moving inside, as if it were trembling. This caused me to wonder if perhaps he was a man of prayer, so I continued to watch him. At the end of the meal one of the old women suddenly became so ill that she began to moan. The master and his wife took her into their bedroom and laid her on the bed. The wife stayed to watch over her while the priest went to get the Presanctified Gifts,[23] just to be on the safe side. The master ordered his carriage and went to fetch the doctor, and the rest of us departed.

I felt a kind of prayerful inner quiet, a deep need to pour out my soul in prayer, and it had already been forty-eight hours since I had experienced any silence or solitude. It felt as if a flood were building up in my

24 Hesychios of Jerusalem: see page 46.

25 St. Ephraim of Syria (ca. 306–ca. 373): A deacon of Syria whose prolific writings include poetry, homilies, treatises, and discourses, and are the most influential of all Christian writings in Syriac (the native language of Syria before it was supplanted by Arabic in the second half of the first millennium C.E.). He is attributed with authorship of the Lenten Prayer of St. Ephraim of Syria, repeated by Orthodox Christians many times each year in the period of Lent, before Easter:

> O Lord and Master of my life,
> Take from me the spirit of sloth, despair, lust of power, and
>   idle talk,
> But grant rather the spirit of chastity, humility, patience, and
>   love to your servant.
> Yes, O Lord and King, grant me to see my own faults, and
>   not to judge my brother and my sister,
> For You are blessed unto ages of ages. Amen.

heart that strained to burst forth and spill out into the rest of my body. The effort to contain it caused a kind of soreness in my heart—a pleasurable feeling—that insistently demanded the peace of silence and could be satisfied only by prayer. Through this it was revealed to me why people who had attained to genuine self-acting interior prayer fled company and took refuge in solitude. I understood also why the venerable Hesychios[24] said that even the most beneficial conversation was idle chatter when taken to excess, just as St. Ephraim of Syria[25] said, "Good speech is silver, but silence is pure gold."

As I thought about all this I walked to the guesthouse, where everyone was resting after the meal. I climbed up to the attic, calmed myself, rested, and prayed a bit. When the beggars had gotten up from their rest, I found the blind man and walked with him just beyond the kitchen garden, where we sat down alone and began to talk.

"For God's sake, would you tell me if you are praying the Jesus prayer for spiritual benefit?"

"I have been praying it unceasingly for quite some time now," he replied.

"And what is your experience of it?"

"Only that I cannot be without the prayer day or night."

"How did God reveal this practice to you? Tell me everything, dear brother."

"Well, you see, I once earned my living as a tailor, traveling to other provinces and villages, making clothing for the peasants.

"One time I happened to spend a longer time in one of the villages, living with a peasant for whose family I was making clothing. On one of the feast days I noticed three books lying near the icon case, and I asked, 'Who in the household knows how to read?' 'No one,' they replied. 'These books were left to us by our uncle, who knew how to read and write.' I picked up one of the books and opened it at random. On one

❖ "Let every pious person continually repeat this Name as a prayer in his mind and with his tongue. Let him always constrain himself to do this while standing, travelling, sitting, resting, speaking, and doing all things. Then he shall find great peace and joy, as those who have occupied themselves with it know from experience. This activity is both for those in worldly life, and for those monks who are in the midst of turmoil. Each one must strive to occupy himself with this prayer, even if to a limited extent only. All, clergy, monks, and laymen, must have this prayer as a guide, practicing it according to their ability."

—Simeon, Archbishop of Thessalonica

26 "Dark water": A colloquial expression for glaucoma.

of the pages I happened to read the following, which I still remember to this day: 'Unceasing prayer is calling always upon the Name of God, whether one is conversing or sitting down, walking, working, or eating, or occupied with any other activity—in all places and at all times one should call upon the Name of God.' After reading this I began to realize that it would be quite convenient for me to do this. So I began to repeat the prayer in a quiet whisper while I sewed, and I found it much to my liking. The others living with me in the hut noticed my behavior and began to ridicule me for it. 'What are you, a sorcerer?' they asked. 'What are you whispering all the time? Are you trying to cast a spell?' So to cover up what I was doing, I stopped moving my lips and began to pray only with my tongue. Eventually I grew so accustomed to the prayer that day and night my tongue would form the words on its own, and this became quite pleasant.

"So I lived this way for quite a while, going from village to village to sew, until all of a sudden I was stricken with blindness. Almost everyone in our family suffers from 'dark water.'[26] When I became poverty-stricken, our guild placed me in an almshouse in Tobolsk, the capital of our province. I was on my way there when the master and mistress urged me to stop over here so they could provide me with a cart that would take me there."

"What was the name of the book you read?" I asked him. "Was it by any chance the *Philokalia*?"

"I do not honestly know; I didn't even look at the title."

I brought my *Philokalia* to him, and in part 4 I found the passage by Patriarch Callistus that the blind man had just quoted from memory. I read it back to him and he cried out, "That's it, that's exactly it! Keep on reading, brother—this is truly wonderful!"

When I got to the line "One should pray with the heart," he began to ply me with questions: "What does this mean?" and "How do you do

❖ "The head and beginning of all virtues is, to the extent possible, unceasing prayer to our Lord Jesus Christ, which is called by way of abbreviation, the Prayer of Jesus. The Apostle says concerning it: 'Pray without ceasing' (1 Thessalonians 5:17). That is, one must call upon the name of God always, whether we be conversing, sitting, walking, working, eating, or doing anything else. At every time and in every place it is fitting to call upon the name of God. For by this means, writes Chrysostom, the temptation of the enemy is consumed. Beat the warriors, says St. John Climacus, with the name of Jesus, and a stronger weapon you shall not find either in heaven or on earth. Prayer is the banishment of sorrow and dejection, the germination of meekness and angerlessness, the offering of joy and thanksgiving; and innumerable good things reacquired through prayer."

—From "Indication of the Most Essential Spiritual Dispositions and Virtues"
by Abbot Nazarius (1735–1809) of Valaam Monastery, near St. Petersburg
(*Little Russian Philokalia,* vol. 2 [Platina, Calif.:
St. Herman Brotherhood, 1983], p. 66)

this?" I told him that all the teachings on the prayer of the heart were provided in detail in this book, the *Philokalia*. He begged me to read the whole thing to him.

"I'll tell you what to do," I said. "When are you leaving for Tobolsk?"

"I am ready to leave at any time," he replied.

"Then let's do this: since I am also planning to head out tomorrow, you and I can travel together, and I can read to you everything concerning the prayer of the heart as we go. I'll also explain how to locate the place of the heart and how to enter into it."

"But what about the cart?" he asked.

"What do we need with a cart? It's really only about a hundred miles to Tobolsk, and we'll go slowly. Think how good it will be for the two of us alone to travel together. It will be much easier for us to talk and read about prayer as we walk." So we agreed.

That evening the master himself came to call us to dinner. After the meal we told him that the blind man and I would be traveling together and that we would not be needing the cart, since it would be easier for us to read the *Philokalia* that way. When he heard this, the master said, "I too enjoyed the *Philokalia*. In fact, I've already written a letter, enclosing some money, which I'll post to St. Petersburg on my way to the courthouse tomorrow. I've asked them to send it to me immediately."

The next day we set off, after warmly thanking our hosts for their love and generous hospitality. They accompanied us along our way for over a half a mile from their house. And thus we parted with them.

The blind man and I walked short distances at a time, from six to ten miles a day. The rest of the time we sat in secluded spots and read from the *Philokalia*. I read to him all that there was on the prayer of the heart, following the order my late starets had indicated to me, beginning with the books of Nicephorus the Solitary, St. Gregory of Sinai, and so on.

❖   "The unceasing practice of interior, mental prayer should be the most desired spiritual occupation, and still more so because it is accessible and convenient during every physical labor and earthly occupation—while tasting food and drink, while walking, while performing common obediences—always and at all times, day and night, provided that the mind and heart heed their interior work. The godly wise fathers, who through experience learned both its sweetness and its power, wrote very much about the mental prayer of Jesus; thus one spirit-bearing man says: 'With the name of Jesus, or with sincere thought on Jesus, a great power is united: it drives away passions, forbids demons, and fills the heart with heavenly stillness and joy.'"

—Abbess Thaisia of Leushino Convent (died 1915), from a letter to one of her nuns (*Letters to a Beginner: On Giving One's Life to God* [Wildwood, Calif.: St. Xenia Press, 1993], p. 96)

How hungrily and how attentively he took in everything, and how it pleased and delighted him! Then he began to ask me questions about prayer that I was not capable of answering. When we had read all the necessary passages from the *Philokalia*, he begged me to actually show him how the mind can find the heart, how to bring the Name of Jesus Christ into it, and how to experience the delightful interior prayer of the heart. I explained the following to him: "You are blind and can see nothing, but are you not able to imagine in your mind that which you once could see with your eyes—a person or some object or one of your limbs, such as a hand or a foot? Are you not able to imagine it as vividly as if you were actually looking at it, and to concentrate and focus even your blind eyes on it?"

"I can do that," said the blind man.

"Well, then, do the same thing, and try to visualize your heart with your mind. Focus your eyes as if you were looking at it, right through the wall of your chest cavity. Try to visualize it as vividly as possible in your mind, and listen to the steady rhythm of its beating. When you have succeeded with this, then begin to repeat the words of the prayer, in accompaniment to each beat of your heart, keeping your eyes focused on it all the while. Thus, with the first beat you will say, verbally or mentally, the word *Lord*; with the second, *Jesus*; with the third, *Christ*; with the fourth, *have mercy*; with the fifth, *on me*. Repeat this over and over again. It should be easy for you, since you have already learned the basics of the prayer of the heart.

"Eventually, when you get used to it, then you can begin to repeat the full Jesus prayer in your heart, in time with a steady rhythm of inhaling and exhaling, as the Fathers taught. As you inhale, you visualize your heart and say, *Lord Jesus Christ*. As you exhale, you say, *have mercy on me!* Do this as much and as often as you can, and soon you will experience a delicate but pleasant soreness in your heart, which will be followed by

❖ "We are taught, when reciting the Jesus prayer, to avoid so far as possible any specific image or picture. In the words of St. Gregory of Nyssa, 'The Bridegroom is present, but he is not seen.' The Jesus prayer is not a form of imaginative meditation upon different incidents in the life of Christ. But, while turning aside from images, we are to concentrate our full attention upon, or rather within, the words. The Jesus prayer is not just a hypnotic incantation but a meaningful phrase, an invocation addressed to another person. Its object is not relaxation but alertness, not waking slumber but living prayer. And so the Jesus prayer is not to be said mechanically but with inward purpose; yet at the same time the words should be pronounced without tension, violence, or undue emphasis. The string round our spiritual parcel should be taut, not left hanging slack; yet it should not be drawn so tight as to cut into the edges of the package."

—Bishop Kallistos Ware, *The Orthodox Way*, p. 164

warmth and a warming tenderness. If you do this, with God's help you will attain to the delightful self-acting interior prayer of the heart. However, as you do all this, guard against mental imaginings and any sort of visions. Reject everything your imagination produces, for the holy Fathers strictly teach that interior prayer must be a visionless exercise, lest one fall into delusion."

The blind man listened attentively to everything and then earnestly began to practice the specified method of prayer, spending an especially long time on it at night when we stopped to rest.

After about five days he began to feel an intense warmth and an indescribably pleasant sensation in his heart, along with a great desire to devote himself continually to this prayer, which was stirring in him a love for Jesus Christ. From time to time he began seeing a light, though he discerned no visible things or objects in it. At times, when he entered into his heart, it seemed to him that a strong flame, like that of a burning candle, would flare up delightfully within his heart and would illuminate him as it rushed up and outward through his throat. This light made it possible for him to see things even at a great distance, which actually did occur on one occasion.

We happened to be walking through a forest, and he was fully and silently absorbed in his prayer. Suddenly he said to me, "What a pity! The church is burning, and look—the bell tower has fallen down."

"Stop making things up," I said. "That's nothing but a temptation. You must quickly banish all thoughts. How can you possibly see what's happening in the city when we're still almost eight miles from it?"

He took my advice, continued praying, and was silent. Toward evening we arrived in the city, and I actually saw several burned-down buildings and a collapsed bell tower, which had stood on wooden pilings. Many people were standing about, amazed that no one had been hurt or killed when the tower collapsed. By my calculation, this tragedy

❖ "When practicing the Jesus prayer, remember that the most important thing of all is humility; then the ability—not the decision only—
always to maintain a keen sense of responsibility toward God, toward
one's spiritual director, toward people, and even things. Remember too
that Isaac of Syria warns us that God's wrath visits all who refuse the
bitter cross of agony, the cross of active suffering, and who, striving
after visions and special graces of prayer, waywardly seek to appropri-
ate the glories of the cross. He also says, 'God's grace comes of itself,
suddenly, without seeing it approach. It comes when the place is clean.'
Therefore, carefully, diligently, constantly clean the place; sweep it with
the broom of humility."

—Starets Macarius of Optina Monastery (died 1860)

occurred exactly at the time the blind man told me about it. So he said to me, "You said I was imagining things, and yet it happened just as I saw it. How can one not love and be grateful to the Lord Jesus Christ, Who manifests His grace to sinners, to the blind and the unwise! I thank you too for teaching me the work of the heart."

"You can love Jesus Christ and be as grateful to him as you want to be," I said, "but beware of accepting visions as direct revelations of grace, because such things can often occur as natural manifestations. The human soul is not absolutely bound by space and matter. It can also see events through darkness and at very great distances, as if they were happening nearby. It is we who do not give power and momentum to this capability in our souls, and we squelch it beneath the bonds of either the carnality of our bodies or our confused thoughts and scattered ideas. Yet, when we focus our attention on the inner self, divert our concentration from everything external, and refine our mind, then the soul finds its truest fulfillment and exercises its highest powers, and this is all quite natural. I heard from my late starets that some of those who don't pray, or who have a certain ability, or who suffer from certain sicknesses are able to see, in the darkest room, an aura of light that radiates out from all things. But what occurs during the prayer of the heart is the direct result of God's grace, and it is so delightful that no tongue can describe it or even compare it to anything at all. All physical sensations are base in comparison to the delightful experience of grace acting within the heart."

My blind friend listened carefully to all this and was even more humbled by it. The prayer continued to increase within his heart, delighting him beyond description. I rejoiced in this with all my heart and earnestly thanked God for granting me to have met such a blessed servant of His.

Finally we arrived in Tobolsk, where I took him to the almshouse.

❖ "Blessed are they who become accustomed to this heavenly activity, for by it they conquer all the temptations of the evil spirits, just as David conquered the proud Goliath. In this way they quench the disorderly desires of the flesh, just as the three youths quenched the flames of the furnace. By means of mental prayer the passions are tamed, just as Daniel tamed the wild beasts. It draws the dew of the Holy Spirit down into the heart, just as the prayers of Elijah brought down rain upon Mt. Carmel. This mental prayer reaches the very throne of God where it is treasured in golden vials and like a censer it gives off a sweet fragrance before the Lord just as St. John the Theologian saw in his revelation: *Four and twenty elders fell down before the Lamb, having every one of them harps, and golden vials full of odours, which are the prayers of saints* (Rev. 5:8). This mental prayer is the light enlightening man's soul and enkindling his heart with the fire of love towards God. It is the chain uniting God to man and man to God. Oh, there is nothing that can compare to the grace of mental prayer! It makes man a constant converser with God. O truly wondrous and most wondrous work! In the body you are with people, but mentally you converse with God.

—St. Gregory Palamas (See page 18)

27 St. John of Karpathos: See page 64.

After kindly parting with him, I left him there and continued on my journey.

For a month I walked slowly, reflecting in depth on how edifying and encouraging the good experiences in life can be. I read the *Philokalia* often to verify all that I had told the blind man of prayer. His example kindled in me zeal, gratitude, and love for the Lord. The prayer of the heart delighted me so much that I thought there could be no one happier than me in the whole world, and I could not imagine how there would be any greater or deeper contentment even in the Kingdom of Heaven. I experienced all this not only within myself, but outwardly as well—everything around me appeared wondrous to me and inspired me with love for and gratitude to God. People, trees, plants, and animals—I felt a kinship with them all and discovered how each bore the seal of the Name of Jesus Christ. At times I felt so light that it was as if I had no body and were not walking but rather joyously floating through the air. At other times I entered so fully into myself that I saw clearly all my inner organs, and this caused me to marvel at the wisdom that went into creating the human body. Sometimes I knew such joy that I felt like a king. At such consoling moments I wished that God would grant me to die soon, so that I could pour myself out in gratitude at His feet in heaven.

Yet, it became apparent to me that my enjoyment of these experiences was tempered or had been regulated by God's will, because I soon began to experience some sort of anxiety and fear in my heart. "I hope this is not another sign of some upcoming disaster or misfortune," I thought. Clouds of thoughts descended upon my mind, and I remembered the words of the blessed John of Karpathos,[27] who said that often the teacher submits to humiliation and suffers misfortune and temptations for those who will benefit from him spiritually. After struggling for a while with such thoughts, I began to pray more earnestly, and the

❖　"The Jesus prayer helps to lift the whole life, body and soul, to a level where the senses and imagination no longer seek for outward change or stimulation, where all is subordinated to the one aim of centering the whole attention of body and soul upon God, in the sense that the world is sought and known in the beauty of God, not God in the beauty of the world."

—Mother Maria of Normamby (1912–1977)

thoughts were banished completely. I was encouraged by this and said to myself, "God's will be done! Anything that Jesus Christ may send my way I am ready to endure for my wretchedness and arrogance—for even those to whom I had recently disclosed the secret of entering the heart and of interior prayer had been prepared directly by God's hidden guidance, before I met them." This thought calmed me, and once again I set off with consolation and with the prayer, feeling even fuller of joy than before.

It rained for about two days and the road had completely turned to mud, so that my legs sank into it and I was barely able to walk. Thus I walked through the steppe and did not come across any human habitation for almost ten miles. At last, toward evening, I came upon a farmhouse right near the road. I was overjoyed and thought to myself, "I can ask to spend the night and rest up here, and I'll accept whatever God sends my way tomorrow morning. Perhaps even the weather will be better."

As I approached I saw a drunken old man wearing an army coat and sitting on a mound of earth by the farmhouse. I bowed to him and said, "Would it be possible to ask someone if I could spend the night here?"

"Who else could let you do that but me?" the old man bellowed. "I'm in charge here! This is a post office, and I'm the postmaster."

"Well, then, Batushka, will you permit me to spend the night here?"

"Do you have a passport? Let me see some legal proof of who you are!"

I gave him my passport, and as he held it he asked, "Well, where's the passport?"

"You're holding it," I replied.

"Oh, well, then—let's go inside the hut."

The postmaster put on his glasses, studied the passport, and said, "It's a legal document, all right. You can stay the night. I'm a good man, you know. Here—I'll even offer you a welcome drink."

❖ "The starets tells the pilgrim that if you keep saying that prayer over and over again—you only have to just do it with your *lips* at first—then eventually what happens, the prayer becomes self-active. Something *happens* after a while. I don't know what, but something happens, and the words get synchronized with a person's heartbeats, and then you're actually praying without ceasing. Which has a really tremendous, mystical effect on your whole outlook. I mean that's the whole *point* of it, more or less. I mean you do it to purify your whole outlook and get an absolutely new conception of what everything's about."

Lane had finished eating. Now as Franny paused again, he sat back and lit a cigarette and watched her face. She was still looking abstractedly ahead of her, past his shoulder, and seemed scarcely aware of his presence.

"But the thing is, the marvelous thing is, when you first start doing it, you don't even have to have faith in what you're doing. I mean even if you're terribly embarrassed about the whole thing, it's perfectly all right. I mean you're not *insulting* anybody or anything. In other words, no one asks you to believe a single thing when you first start out. You don't even have to think about what you're saying, the starets said. All you have to do in the beginning is quantity. Then, later on, it becomes quality by itself. On its own power or something. He says that any name of God—any name at all—has this peculiar, self-active power of its own, and it starts working after you've sort of started it up."

—From Franny Glass's explanation of *The Way of a Pilgrim*
to her boyfriend in J.D. Salinger's novel *Franny and Zooey*

"I've never had a drink in my entire life," I replied.

"Well, no matter! In that case, have dinner with us, at least." We sat down at the table with him and his cook, a young peasant woman who was herself also a little drunk. They sat me down to eat with them, and they fought with each other throughout the meal. By the end of the meal they were fighting seriously. Then the postmaster went off to sleep in the pantry while the woman began clearing the table, washing the cups and spoons, and cursing the old man.

I sat for a while and decided it would be some time before she calmed down, so I said, "Matushka, where could I sleep for the night? I'm exhausted from my journey."

"Here, dear father, I'll make you up a bed." She pulled another bench up to the one near the front window, covered it with a felt blanket, and put a pillow at the end. I lay down and shut my eyes and pretended to sleep. She continued to putter around for a while until at last she had cleaned up. She put out the fire and had started coming over to me when suddenly the entire window in the front corner of the house—the frame, the glass, and all—came showering down with a terrible crash. The entire hut shook, and from just outside the window there came a sickening groan, shouting, and loud scuffling noises. The peasant woman sprang back in terror and jumped into the middle of the room, where she went crashing down on the floor.

I jumped up half conscious, thinking that the very ground under me had split wide open. Then I saw two coach drivers entering the hut. They carried between them a man so covered with blood that you couldn't even see his face, which frightened me even more. He was a royal courier who had been on his way there for a change of horses. His coach driver had miscalculated the turn into the gates, the carriage pole had knocked out the window, and, as there was a ditch in front of the house, the wagon had overturned. The courier was thrown clear, and

St. Nikodemos of Mount Athos, compiler of the Philokalia

he deeply gouged his head against a sharp stake in the ground that was propping up the earthen mound that served as a bench. He demanded some water and wine to wash his wound with, and after bathing it with some of the wine, he drank a glass of it himself. Then he shouted, "Get the horses!"

I went over to him and said, "Sir, how can you travel when you're in such pain?"

"A royal courier has no time to be sick," he replied and galloped away. The coach drivers dragged the unconscious peasant woman to the stove in the corner of the room and covered her with a rug.

"She's only in shock from being so frightened. She'll come out of it," the postmaster said. He then had another drink to ease his hangover and went back to bed, leaving me by myself.

Soon the peasant woman got up and began to pace back and forth, from one corner of the room to the other, until finally she walked out of the hut. I said my prayers and realized how exhausted I was, but I was able to catch a bit of sleep just before dawn.

In the morning I took my leave of the postmaster and set off. As I walked I offered up my prayer with faith, hope, and gratitude to the Father of all blessings and consolations, Who had kept me safe in the midst of this disaster.

Six years after this incident I was passing a women's monastery and stopped in their church to pray. The abbess was most hospitable to pilgrims and invited me inside after the Liturgy, asking that some tea be brought to me. Then some unexpected guests arrived for the abbess, and she went to greet them, leaving me alone with her nuns. The one who was pouring my tea struck me as a truly humble woman, so I could not resist asking her, "Mother, have you been in this monastery a long time?"

"Five years," she replied. "I was out of my mind when they brought

28 Tonsure: The rite of becoming a monk or nun, in which bits of hair are clipped from the head as a sign of the beginning of a new life.

29 The incident referred to is found in the book of Tobit (not found in Protestant Bibles). Tobit, an Israelite living in capitivity in Nineveh, sends his son Tobias on a mission to retrieve some money he has deposited in the city of Media. Throughout his journey, fraught with tribulation and adventure, Tobias is accompanied by the archangel Raphael, disguised in the form of a man, who protects him along the way.

me here. But God was merciful to me, and the mother abbess let me stay and be tonsured."**28**

"What caused you to go out of your mind?" I asked.

"I was in shock from a terrifying experience that happened while I was working at a post office. It was at night, and I was sleeping when some horses knocked out one of the windows, and I went mad from fear. For an entire year my family took me from one holy shrine to another, and it was only here that I was healed."

Upon hearing this my soul rejoiced and glorified God, Who so wisely orders all things for the good.

When I finished relating my stories, I said to my spiritual father, "For God's sake, forgive me—I have talked for too long! The holy Fathers say that even spiritual conversation is vainglory if it is unrestrained. It is now time for me to go and join my companion for the trip to Jerusalem. Pray for me, a wretched sinner, that the Lord in His infinite mercy will grant me a good journey."

"My beloved brother in Christ, with all my soul I wish that the grace of God, abounding with love, will bless your path and go with you on your journey, just as the angel Raphael accompanied Tobias!"**29**

Glossary ■

Akathist: An ancient form of Orthodox hymnody, addressed to Christ, to the Virgin, or to saints. Akathists are composed of fourteen sections and are usually hymns of praise.

Altar: The area of the church where the clergy stand and where most of the solemn parts of the Divine Liturgy are celebrated.

Ascetic: One who practices asceticism.

Asceticism: The practice of self-denial or self-discipline as a means to spiritual attainment.

Batushka (Russian): "Little Father." An affectionate term for an older, respected man, especially a priest.

Canon: An ancient form of Orthodox hymnody, usually consisting of eight odes. *See also* Akathist.

Chotki (Russian; Greek: *komvoskoini*): An Orthodox rosary or prayer-rope used in counting prayers, especially the Jesus prayer.

Divine Liturgy: The Divine Liturgy of St. John Chrysostom. The form of the Eucharistic service used in the Orthodox Church on all Sundays and feast days, with few exceptions.

Eucharist: From the Greek for "thanksgiving," the principle service of celebration in Christian worship, at which Jesus' last meal with his disciples is commemorated, and at which the faithful receive communion: bread and wine that are considered to mystically represent the body and blood of Christ. The service also includes readings from the Bible and the singing of hymns.

Hesychasm: The Orthodox Church's mystical tradition of prayer, based on the practice of the Jesus prayer.

Hesychast: One who practices hesychasm.

Icon: A holy image, usually painted on wood, such as adorn Orthodox churches. Icons are also found in most pious homes, usually in a special corner, the "icon corner."

Iconostasis: The screen, covered with icons, that separates the altar from the nave in Orthodox churches.

Lavra: An ancient term for a monastery, that became a title given to certain large Russian monasteries. In the pilgrim's time there were nine monasteries in Russia that bore the title *lavra*, including the Lavra of the Kiev Caves.

Matins: The morning service of the daily cycle of twelve services performed in monasteries. It is also celebrated in ordinary parish churches.

Matushka (Russian): "Little Mother." Term most often used to refer to a priest's wife, but also sometimes used as an affectionate term for any respected woman.

Menaion: The set of service books that contains the daily elements of Orthodox church services for the entire year.

Narthex: The church entrance, or vestibule.

Nave: The main body of a church, where the congregration stands.

Old Believers: Common name for the Russian sect that separated from the Orthodox Church in the seventeenth century over issues of liturgical reform.

Orthodox Church: General term for the churches of Greece, the Mediterranean, and Eastern Europe that broke with the Roman Catholic Church in the eleventh century, and whose spirituality is characterized by hesychasm. Orthodox Christianity is the prevalent faith in Greece, Cyprus, Russia, Ukraine, Romania, Bulgaria, and large parts of Yugoslavia, and is a primary Christian presence in Albania, Syria, Lebanon, and throughout the Middle East. There are significant minority Orthodox communities in Poland, the Czech Republic, and Finland, as well as in Western Europe and in North and South America. It is also referred to as the Eastern Orthodox Church, and includes the churches known in the United States as Russian, Greek, and Antiochian Orthodox.

Philokalia (Greek: "Love of Beauty"): The great anthology of Eastern Orthodox writings on prayer, covering a period of eleven centuries. In Russian it is called *Dobrotolubiye* ("Love of the Good").

Prostration (Russian: *poklon*): A deep bow in which the worshiper kneels and touches his or her forehead to the floor.

Schema monk or schema nun (Russian: *skhmnik* or *skhimnitsa*): A monk or nun who has taken permanent and binding monastic vows.

Slavonic: The liturgical language of the Russian church and of all other Orthodox churches in Slavic lands. It was invented, along with the Cyrillic alphabet, by the Byzantine missionary saints Cyril and Methodius, in the ninth century and is still in use in Russian churches today.

Skete: A small monastic settlement, often dependent upon a larger monastery.

Starets (Russian; plural: *startsi*): An elder or spiritual father, usually a monk, to whom Orthodox Christians may look as a guide.

Theotokos (Greek; Russian: *Bogoroditsa*): "God-Bearer." A very common epithet for the Virgin Mary among the Orthodox, assigned to her at the Church's Third Ecumenical Council in 431.

Vespers: The evening service from the monastic cycle of services. It is also celebrated outside monasteries, in ordinary parish churches.

Suggestions for Further Reading ◼

Brianchaninov, Ignatius. *On the Prayer of Jesus*. Translated by Father Lazarus. London: John M. Watkins, 1965. One of the most valuable books on the practice of the Jesus prayer in English. Bishop Brianchaninov's book, written in the mid-nineteenth century, provides inspiring and practical advice. It is currently, unfortunately, out of print, but it can and should be tracked down in libraries and used bookstores.

Chariton, Igumen, ed. *The Art of Prayer: An Orthodox Anthology*. Translated by E. Kadloubovsky and E. M. Palmer. London: Faber & Faber, 1997. A classic of Russian spirituality. Contains numerous texts on prayer by Theophan the Recluse (see page 14) as well as pieces by both Greek and Russian spiritual writers.

Kadloubovsky, E., and G. E. H. Palmer, trans. *Writings from the Philokalia on the Prayer of the Heart*. London: Faber & Faber, 1992. First published in the 1950s, this anthology—translated into English from the Russian translation by Bishop Theophan the Recluse—could be called the "portable *Philokalia*," as it contains all the most essential and accessible texts on the prayer of the heart, in exactly the order the pilgrim's starets recommended approaching them.

Kovalevsky, Pierre. *Saint Sergius and Russian Spirituality*. Crestwood, N.Y.: St. Vladimir's Seminary Press, 1976. A popularly written, illustrated study of Russian spirituality, beginning with the life of St. Sergius of Radonezh, founder of the famous Holy Trinity Monastery at Zagorsk, near Moscow. A good overview of the spirituality found in *The Way of a Pilgrim*.

Meyendorff, John. *St. Gregory Palamas and Orthodox Spirituality*. Crestwood, N.Y.: St. Vladimir's Seminary Press, 1959. A popular, illustrated examination of hesychasm in Orthodox spirituality and of its fourteenth-century proponent and defender.

Monk of the Eastern Church, A. *The Jesus Prayer*. Crestwood, N.Y.: St. Vladimir's Seminary Press, 1987.

Rose, Father Seraphim, trans. *The Northern Thebaid: Monastic Saints of the Russian North*. Platina, Calif.: St. Herman of Alaska Brotherhood, 1995. With its charming period illustrations and text taken from popular Russian saints' lives, this book gives one a very good feel for Russian piety in the period when the pilgrim was writing.

Smith, T. Allan, trans. *The Pilgrim's Tale*. Edited with an introduction by Aleksei Pentkovsky. Mahwah, N.J.: Paulist Press, 1999. This most recent translation of *The Way of a Pilgrim* contains a fascinating introduction to the history of the text.

Stinissen, Winifred. *Praying the Name of Jesus: The Ancient Wisdom of the Jesus Prayer*. Ligouri, Mo.: Liguori Publications, 1999.

Ware, Bishop Kallistos. *The Orthodox Way*. Crestwood, N.Y.: St. Vladimir's Seminary Press, 1995. A popular approach to Orthodox spirituality that looks at all the approaches to God—as mystery, as prayer, and so forth—with a wealth of inspiring quotations.

Ware, Timothy. *The Orthodox Church*. New York: Penguin USA, 1993. The best short introduction to the Orthodox faith, history, theology, and practice.

Zaleski, Irma. *Living the Jesus Prayer*. New York: Continuum, 1998. A short and simple introduction.